General Editor: J. R. MULRYNE

All's Well That Ends Well

All's Well
That Ends Well

J. L. STYAN

Manchester
University Press

© J. L. STYAN 1984

Published by
Manchester University Press

Oxford Road, Manchester M13 9PL

and
51 Washington Street, Dover, New Hampshire

British Library cataloguing in publication data

Styan, J. L.
  All's well that end well.—(Shakespeare in
  performance)
  1. Shakespeare, William. All's well that ends well
  2. Shakespeare, William—Stage history
  I. Title   II. Series
  792.9'5   PR2801

  ISBN 0-7190-0959-6

Library of Congress cataloging in publication data

Styan, J. L.
  All's well that ends well.
  (Shakespeare in performance)
  Bibliography: p.
  Includes index.
  1. Shakespeare, William, 1564-1616. All's well that
ends well. 2. Shakespeare, William, 1564-1616—Stage
history. I. Shakespeare, William, 1564-1616. All's
well that ends well. II. Title. III. Series.
PR2801.S8 1983   822.3'3   83-11246
ISBN 0-7190-0959-6

Typeset by Graphicraft Typesetters Ltd, Hong Kong

Printed in Hong Kong
by Wing King Tong Co., Ltd

CONTENTS

SERIES EDITOR'S PREFACE

The study of Shakespeare's plays as scripts for performance in the theatre has grown in recent years to become a major interest for many University, College and Sixth-form students and their teachers. The aim of the present series is to assist this study by describing how certain of Shakespeare's texts have been realised in production.

The series is not concerned to provide theatre histories. Rather, each contributor has selected a small number of productions of a particular play and studied them comparatively. The productions, often from different periods, countries and media, have been chosen because they are significant interpretations in their own right, but also because they represent something of the range and variety of possible interpretations of the play in hand. In this way, it is hoped that students' and theatregoers' own reading and understanding of a text will be enlarged. They should also begin to appreciate some of the ways in which practical considerations influence the meanings a production incorporates: the stage the actor plays on, the acting company, the player's own physique and abilities, stage-design and theatre-tradition, the expectations of a particular audience.

Any study of a Shakespeare text will reveal only a small proportion of the text's potential meanings. I hope that the effect of this series will be to encourage a kind of reading that is receptive to the ever-varying discoveries theatre interpretation provides.

J. R. Mulryne

PREFATORY NOTE

My sincere thanks go to the Librarians at the Shakespeare Centre, Stratford-upon-Avon and the Colindale Newspaper Collection of the British Library for their help in finding the material for this book; to Cheri Peters for her contribution in preparing an early draft; and to John Bouchard and the Rice University players whose excellent production and discussion of *All's Well* unravelled some of my thinking at an important moment at its inception.

I have made a point of using documentary evidence for the details of the productions I describe, and of not disclosing which of them I have seen myself.

All quotations from the play are from Peter Alexander's *William Shakespeare: the Complete Works* (London and Glasgow, 1951), unless otherwise indicated.

JLS
1981

PART I

Issues of performance

A play without a past

All's Well That Ends Well is for us virtually a new play, and in this it is not unlike another problem comedy that has only recently found an audience, *Troilus and Cressida.* The 'indelicacy' of the central story, in which a woman pursues a man all the way into his bed, has ensured that the play has had no theatrical history worth mentioning until a few years ago. It therefore comes to us largely unencumbered by the débris of stage tradition, and because of the ambiguities surrounding the woman in question, it also comes with few of the critical preconceptions which can stultify productions and performances (not counting its reputation for commercial disaster). If we hold that a play lives and grows for as long as it is being played and seen, in the case of *All's Well* we are privileged to be midwives to its birth.

In spite of Hazlitt's perverse verdict in his *Characters of Shakespeare's Plays* (1817) that *All's Well* was 'one of the most pleasing of our author's comedies', there were few who subsequently agreed with him. In 1929 Arthur Quiller-Couch concluded his introduction to the New Cambridge edition by saying, 'In fine, we hold this play to be one of Shakespeare's worst'; and in the same edition Harold Child began his story of the production of the play with the chilling comment, 'The stage-history of this comedy is brief and inglorious'. At that date he was right. There was no record of a production of *All's Well* before 1741, when it saw the light for five performances; and then in 1742 Peg Woffington as Helena fell and fainted on the stage, while the King of France died of a cold in the head soon after. However, the play was sustained for several performances after 1746 by the Harlequin talents of Harry Woodward as Parolles, but it flopped under John Philip Kemble in 1794 and under his younger brother Charles in 1811. It emerged again at Covent Garden in 1832 as an opera, even though *The Theatrical Observer* found its plot 'objectionable to modern refinement' (17 October), and it achieved eleven performances under Phelps at Sadler's Wells in 1852 in spite of the judgment by *The Athenaeum* that 'the manners represented are exceedingly gross' (4 September). Doubtless a Victorian Helena should more properly have had a fit of the vapours at the mention of a fistula. Thereafter the play sank into oblivion for more than half a century, unheard of in late Victorian England or America. It took on perfunctory and fitful life with the development of the Stratford-upon-Avon festivals, under F. R. Benson in 1916, W. Bridges-Adams in 1922 and Ben Iden Payne in 1935, and made a fleeting appearance under Robert Atkins at the Old Vic in 1921. Joseph Price tells this miserable history in his book, *The Unfortunate Comedy.*

By the middle of this century the play had all but been written off as an acceptable offering for the commercial stage. Its content and style had virtually defeated all attempts to revive it successfully, and it is merely amusing to read the obligatory comments that surround the earlier productions. At best, Benson's work in 1916 had attained the 'success of curiosity', since *The Birmingham Daily Post* believed the play had 'never been performed in Shakespeare's native place' (1 May). After the Old Vic production of 1921, *The Observer* echoed the long chorus of detractors by declaring that the play 'was very nearly the worst play its distinguished author ever wrote' (4 December), and after the Birthday performance at Stratford-upon-Avon in 1922, *The Morning Post* decided that it was no more than 'a scamped pot-boiler'. *The Sunday Times* seemed to settle the matter once and for all by immortalising in print the stern verdict,

> This is one of Shakespeare's earliest and worst efforts. It was
> misconceived, misbegotten and misnamed. Its ending is far from
> well. It finishes deplorably. What possible satisfaction can there
> be to anyone in the reunion of such an ignominious pair? A more
> unsympathetic hero and heroine it is impossible to find in the
> whole gallery of Shakespearean portraits. (4 December 1921)

Of course, *All's Well* is not now taken to be an early play, but to
fall in the mature sequence of *Hamlet, Troilus and Cressida* and
Measure for Measure. It is another of Shakespeare's extraordinary experiments for the stage, but in spite of Kenneth Muir's
belief in his *Shakespeare's Sources* of 1957 that 'it is a play that
acts much better than it reads' (p, 101), such derogatory
sentiments continued to be expressed. In his introduction to the
New Arden edition of 1959, G. K. Hunter was still troubled by the
reasons why the play was not often read or performed (p. xxix),
and in *Shakespeare Quarterly* in 1964, Jay Halio continued to
write of it as if it were 'a failure' (p. 33).

One reason is that the play has more than its share of the
seamier side of Elizabethan wit, and the text has usually been
cut to spare our blushes. The collation of sixty-three acting
editions and prompt-books of *All's Well* in William Halstead's
Shakespeare as Spoken indicates that the scissors did heavy duty
in this play. The unmentionable discussion on virginity
(I.1.104-74) was never heard until recently, and throughout the
nineteenth century lines were obliterated when they seemed too
explicit to some manager. Lines lost in this way included
Bertram's to Diana, 'give thyself unto my sick desires' (IV.2.35),
and Diana's riddle,

> He knows himself my bed he hath defil'd;
> And at that time he got his wife with child.
> Dead though she be, she feels her young one kick;
> So there's my riddle: one that's dead is quick.
> (V.3.294-7)

And until recently Helena was sanitised out of recognition,
together with much of the bed trickery of III.5, III.7 and IV.4.
John Philip Kemble began the Victorian tradition of making the
production of the ring, and not the baby, the only condition
named in Bertram's letter of III.2.55.

Coherence in the story itself must have been imperceptible,
and so the audience for Benson's production found: *The
Birmingham Daily Post* actually suggested that the play should

be done as 'a wild and jolly farce' like *The Taming of the Shrew*, but with 'a female Petruchio' to tame her husband (1 May 1916). Worse, reviewers and commentators were unable to identify a characteristic tone and idiom for the play: *All's Well* appeared to lack even the dark comic unity of *Measure for Measure*. Thus, in the years since World War II, Michael Benthall treated the play as a fairy tale, with Claire Bloom's beautiful Helena blessed with the long blonde tresses of a Cinderella. Noël Willman arbitrarily introduced a new shade of revulsion by making his clown Lavache a dwarf and a hunchback. John Barton sugared over the bitterness in the story a little with the fey charms and big round eyes of Estelle Kohler as a precocious schoolgirl Helena.

Nevertheless, by the time of Barton's production of 1967, *All's Well* had become another play. *The Birmingham Mail* found it 'one of the season's pleasures' and Herbert Kretzmer in *The Daily Express* could represent the popular verdict with a statement that would have been unbelievable a hundred years before: 'It is a lovely and a loving play and I adored every moment of it' (both 2 June). In 1981 the television production by Elijah Moshinsky proved to be one of the most successful of the BBC's series, a spell-binding experience for millions of viewers, and Trevor Nunn's production at Stratford-upon-Avon later that year was the most assured of the season, sending its audience home, in Michael Billington's words, 'filled with a radiant over-powering happiness' (*The Guardian Weekly*, 18 July 1982). What had happened? The change could possibly be put down to the broadening of public taste in matters of sex. But by the test of performance stylistic virtues in the play had also begun to reveal themselves.

In a nutshell, two elements in the play had governed its presentation and reception over the years, both mutually dependent: its controversial content and its unusual style. In this century, time and the change in social taste, with a greater understanding of the realism in character and situation, have taken care of much of the first, and developments in the production of Shakespeare, a more open stage and a more imaginative theatre, have demonstrated the second. Our play may today claim a more secure place in the theatrical canon, some 350 years after it was written.

Before the war, the newly-appointed director of the Stratford Memorial Theatre in 1935, Ben Iden Payne, had introduced a 'fit-up' Elizabethan 'inner stage' set behind a traverse curtain. This curtain was hung between two pillars which also served to support a penthouse roof erected inside the proscenium arch. He thus in part rejected the old sense of illusion and achieved a new pace and rhythm in the action. However, he was not able to escape the limitations of the proscenium arch, and lacked the spatial freedom which was to mark post-war productions: *The Yorkshire Post* decided that the 'curtains constantly travelling across a false proscenium arch' resulted only in 'swiftness, continuity, and monotony' (24 April). The production of the play by Tyrone Guthrie on the newly constructed thrust stage of the Stratford, Ontario Festival Theatre in 1953 now appears to have been a watershed in the history of the play. It was a stage, Guthrie wrote in his autobiography, *A Life in the the Theatre*, 'planned upon the theory that illusion is not the aim of performance' (p. 301). This production was revived and adjusted for the proscenium stage of the Memorial Theatre in 1959, and managed to retain some of its original spirit of non-illusion. The Guthrie production proved to be the one which opened up the play, identified a unity of theme and style, and suggested possibilities for future productions. In his use of Ontario's open stage Guthrie may have managed to recapture something of the style that Shakespeare conceivably intended for the Globe.

Guthrie's contribution to the play was a free choreography of such imaginative range that the play's quality of fantasy and wit could be mixed with its element of realism in characterization. In *Shakespeare's Problem Plays* E. M. W. Tillyard observed that 'Shakespeare had at his call a rather clumsy and heightened style in rhyme which he used from time to time to mark certain passages in his plays violently off from the rest', but in *All's Well* he considered that Shakespeare in using this style was 'deliberately evading drama and substituting ritual and cloudy incantation' (pp. 101-2) when Helena cured the King. Tillyard was closer than he knew to the sense of ritual conferred on the play in performance by the couplets, and Guthrie made them work, not only for the scenes of curing the King and choosing a husband, but in order to promote the magical side of Helena's role.

John Barton, working in Stratford-upon-Avon and the Aldwych in a comparable spirit of non-illusion in 1967 and 1968, had his designer Timothy O'Brien superimpose a simple wooden stage on the main one and backed it with a pavilion. And he also found an appreciative audience for a less romantic analysis of class distinction and the sexual relationship in the play. So it was that, under Barton, a play that had once been pronounced the least attractive of Shakespeare's comedies was played for its wit and wisdom, and was found to be 'much the most enjoyable of Shakespeare's comedies' (B. A. Young in *The Financial Times*), and 'no longer a problem play', but 'delightfully tongue-in-cheek' (Eric Shorter in *The Daily Telegraph*); this was '*All's Well* without a dark side' (Henry Popkin in *The Times*, all 18 January 1968). Style and content were working together.

Romance or realism?

There will, of course, never be a definitive way to present the play, and it is helpful to recognise the range of styles seen in production. In its comparatively short life-span, all of the play's dramatic and theatrical ingredients have been perceived differently, whether setting, character, costume, mood or atmosphere. The play has been a vehicle for a tale of romantic love or for a more realistic psychological study, a polarisation usefully advanced by Joseph Price in his book. No matter whether the emphasis was on woman's role in society, honour between men and women, the sexual double standard, the effects of class differences or the conflicting viewpoints of youth and age, it could be treated either romantically or realistically. A realistic production tends to see Bertram as his own man and honest according to his lights, and Helena as less maidenly, a woman prepared to break the conventions of courtship and female modesty. The romantic view finds Bertram at fault, but worthy of redemption, and implicitly applauds the commitment and steadfastness of Helena's love as it endures all vicissitudes.

For many years the romantic interpretation dictated the decoration of the stage, its scenery and costumes, probably in response to the scholarship which identified the play's sources as those of the folk-tale. In Samuel Phelps's production at Sadler's Wells in 1852-3, a 'picturesque' presentation made it possible for *John Bull* to find Helena 'a love-sick fool' doting on a 'scoundrel' (4 September 1852). Bridges-Adams's Bertram of 1922, Maurice Colbourne, looked 'exactly like an armoured knight from a Burne-Jones window—a figure too beautiful to be taken seriously' (*The Birmingham Mail*, 24 April). Michael Benthall's 1953 production at Edinburgh and the Old Vic went as far in this direction as the mirthlessness of Helena's story would allow, setting the stage with Osbert Lancaster's pretty castellations and flowery gardens, brightly coloured like a child's picture-book. Encouraged by the element of fantasy in the plot, Benthall's Countess (Fay Compton) appeared like an ancient crone, and the King of France (Laurence Hardy) wore his crown awry and had comic fainting fits. To match Claire Bloom's lovely blonde Helena, John Neville's Bertram was a debonair young rascal whose gaiety made seduction fun.

By contrast, the most solemnly realistic setting yet seen was that of David Myerscough-Jones for television in 1981. It suited the medium well. Rousillon and Paris were depicted after the fashion of a warm seventeenth-century painting by Vermeer, suggesting a quiet domestic interior or a simple royal antechamber, with a Dutch kitchen for the Florentine Widow and a Dutch alehouse for the soldiery on campaign. Reviewing the production for *Drama*, Michael Ratcliffe ransacked the Caravaggiesque paintings of Holland and France for comparisons ('glowing with light and rich in darkness'): Pieter de Hooch and Georges de la Tour ('all busy women's heads against candlelight'), the great burgher-groups of Rembrandt and Hals for the courtiers round the King's bed, and 'Celia Johnson's delectable Countess, a lovely wise old face framed by a white ruff, was Margareta van Tripp sprung to life' (no. 140, p. 45). The camera found sly and unusual perspectives, and looked intimately through real doorways and windows. Mirrors gave extra depth to the scene, so that Rousillon became a labyrinth of rooms and corridors. Faces caught in close-up, and the glow of flickering firelight emphasised the personal relationships between members of the family, suggested their unspoken thoughts and lent a shadowy realism to the scene.

The Guthrie productions seemed to have it both ways. Working with the impersonal wooden columns and steps of the architectural stage at Stratford, Ontario, he and his designer, Tanya Moiseiwitsch, chose the *fin de siècle* of Edwardian England, the Kaiser's Germany and *Merry Widow* Paris, the twilight years before the Great War. The period was not so modern as to deny the play its timelessness, and just modern enough to take it out of the category of a costume piece. Alec Guiness as the King was elegant in a quilted dressing-gown, pushed in a wheelchair and surrounded by a dashing court of exquisitely turned-out young men in dinner dress or formal regimentals, a court that was romantic and at the same time threatened. The world of Renaissance honour translated well into one of twentieth-century monocles and boiled-shirt formality, and Guthrie's characters were real people conscious of class and propriety. Helena (Irene Worth in Canada and Zoe Caldwell at Stratford-upon-Avon) was first seen in austere black, her hair done in a bun, suggesting the urgency and seriousness of the part: she was the Shavian new woman.

The theatre had waited half a century to take up Bernard Shaw's idea of Helena's modernity as a 'lady doctor' not too squeamish to cure a fistula. In *Our Theatres in the Nineties*, he reported that he had seen only a travesty of the play when it was produced by the Irving Dramatic Club at St George's Hall in 1895, a production which had omitted anything that might offend: 'the whole play was vivisected, and the fragments mutilated' (vol. I, p. 29). Shaw wrote of 'the exquisite tenderness and impulsive courage' with which Helena replaced the patience of a medieval Griselda, and she seemed to speak for the feminist cause. She is of course too rich in feeling to be a Shavian predator, for her chief thought when Bertram goes to war is for his safety; but Shaw was looking for the more incisive, sweet-and-sour mixture found in the play.

This flavour was tasted again in Noël Willman's production of 1955. In spite of the peacock silks and slashes, and the fine white lace collars of Mariano Andreu's Louis XIII costumes, this stately production newly emphasised the sexual issues and social pressures in the play, presenting a solemn Helena in Joyce Redman as a vulnerable middle-class girl in a male environment. More pain was felt by the two Helenas of the Barton productions of 1967 and 1968, Estelle Kohler more brazen in the former and Lynn Farleigh more smitten in the latter. Timothy O'Brien caught a mood of melancholy in the tones of his Caroline costumes and décor, and, confined by the small wooden stage erected on the main stage, the eye took in a less decorative image of the action: in *The Birmingham Post* J. C. Trewin reported that the director 'let the play speak unhampered in as simple and as gravely dignified a framework as I remember' (2 June 1967). It appeared to belong to no particular place or time, and the scene was set for a stark confrontation between Helena and Bertram, and for an unromantic analysis of sex and class in the explicit spirit of a Strindberg. Peter Lewis of *The Daily Mail* asked, 'Who needs a wife because she has a magic touch with a fistula?' (2 June 1967).

The Trevor Nunn production of 1981/1982 worked to strike a similar balance between the romantic and the real. Set with much particularity in the Edwardian period, one of the scenes in the play actually suggested a World War I advanced dressing station not far behind the lines as the guns flashed and roared. Yet John Gunter's highly adaptable set, a glass conservatory supported by white pillars and white iron tracery, serving now for a palatial Rousillon in the country, now for a plush club in Paris, now for a Florentine café, managed to capture the twilight atmosphere of that idealised period too, while the nostalgic theme of Guy Woolfenden's Rousillon waltz tune returned repeatedly to hint at memories of the past and dreams of the future. The production thus moved on two levels, identified by Michael Billington in *The Guardian Weekly* as those of 'a realistic fairytale', a matter of 'pure theatrical alchemy' (29 November 1981).

In these later productions the weight shifted from Bertram's weakness to Helena's strength, and as long as Bertram had no need to be seen in some way heroically, the intensity at the heart of their relationship was felt. In Stratford, Connecticut in 1959, John Houseman had Nancy Wickwire play Helena as an older woman, thus emphasising her tragedy by raising the odds against a successful outcome. In Stratford, Ontario in 1977, also dressed in Louis XIII period, David Jones's anniversary production underlined the realities of war by displaying racks of weapons and equipping the forces of the Duke of Florence with 'sinister black breastplates and plumes', with his officers in 'the sombre furs of a bitter winter campaign' (Roger Warren's words in *Shakespeare Survey* 31, p. 145). All this set off the agony of Martha Henry's very particular psychological need for Bertram, and provided a most urgent reading of her part. Only television's Angela Down, drab and unsmiling, was in more pain throughout the play.

Nevertheless, the challenge of style in *All's Well* cannot be met by giving it over to tragedy, any more than it can be played merely for comedy: the cutting edge comes from whetting the one against the other. The broad, farcical elements which Guthrie's huge comic talent introduced into the Parolles scenes, for example, were in raw contrast with the pathetic story of Helena's unrequited love. These elements surprised and annoyed some by their frivolessness, but they delighted others by expanding the comedy and distancing the action of the whole play. Guthrie encouraged Parolles and the soldiery in a clown act which recalled the antics of Fred Karno's army. Alan Brien, who was strong in disapproval, described the effect in *The Spectator*:

> The Duke of Florence is greeting the French lords who are to fight for him. Mr Guthrie manages to make this an enormous show-piece, fit centre for any Sunday night spectacular at the Palladium. The comic soldiers in baggy shorts, black socks and berets are lined up under a blazing sky by the side of a ruined desert viaduct. The Duke of Florence, a goateed parody of General Smuts, dodders along the line with his officers falling over him every time he halts to peer at a mysterious medal. When he turns suddenly his sword becomes entangled between the legs of his staff officer. When he tries to make a speech from the top of an observation tower, the microphone gets a fit of metallic coughing. When he attempts to salute the flag, it slides slowly down the post again. (24 April 1959)

It was not that Guthrie saw the play as standing in need of additional comic business, but that the wit present in the original (and the Parolles plot is as outrageous as anything in Shakespearian comedy) should lift the tone of the play and work for a contemporary audience. In *The Observer* Harold Clurman considered that such Gargantuan clowning served Shakespeare well:

> I cannot say which is the more impressive: Guthrie's mockery of the military (modern style) and his kidding of the court, or the atmosphere of glamorous shadow he has created, the opulent disease which seems to hover over the king's council and festivities. The figures at these moments, for all their comic absurdity, are made to appear part of a puppet world soon destined to crumble into dust. (26 April 1959)

As the play moved to its close, the comedy of catching out both Parolles and Bertram made the women of the play appear to redress the imbalance of the sexes and seem more wise than the men. Even the joyful humiliation of Parolles can become pathetic, and when Bertram is thoroughly put down, the irony must strike the audience as nicely tongue-in-cheek. Harold Hobson did not believe that Guthrie surrendered his respect for Shakespeare's rhythms, but mounted

> certain phrases of the play, such as the terrible line about the dark house and the detested wife, so that they leap out from the background of his multifarious invention with more than the joy of recognition ... Mr Guthrie's elaborate decorations of the text work with the play, and not against it. They do not assail, but reinforce the effects implicit in the words. (*The Sunday Times*, 26 April 1959)

All's Well is neither Gilbert and Sullivan, nor Ibsen and Strindberg, but mature Shakespearian comedy, in which the painfully human side of the story of Helena's unrequited love and Bertram's inadequacy emerges along with the comedy inherent in their situation.

Sensitive topics

In *All's Well* the hero does not chase his wife; he runs away from her—a reversal of expectations, and not altogether a pleasant one. Moreover, Shakespeare introduced some provocative changes when he took up William Painter's *Palace of Pleasure* and its story of Giletta and Beltramo. Giletta was wealthy, but Shakespeare reduced Helena to poverty, making the difference in social status between herself and Bertram more stark. Giletta had many suitors for her hand in marriage, where Helena had none, thus making her seem far more single-minded in the chase. Painter's King of France did not want Giletta to marry Beltramo, considering that she was aiming too high above her rank; Shakespeare had his King order Bertram to marry Helena, thus showing him caught in the trap. When Giletta returned home after curing the King, she managed Beltramo's estate for several months, but Shakespeare had Helena pursue Bertram immediately and reveal herself as a much more determined girl.

The story of the play itself offers a series of moral shocks and challenges to its audience, even the Elizabethans, as a bare summary of the plot reminds us. The orphaned and penurious daughter of a doctor is brought up by a Countess, and has the misfortune of falling in love with her son the Count: the difficulties of the female unable to convey her intimate feelings are immediately apparent, and differences of social class serve only to aggravate them. When the King is known to be dying of a fatal disease, the girl offers to cure him if he will grant her the husband of her choice: can even her skill in medicine excuse such a request in our eyes? Be that as it may, she succeeds in curing the King and chooses the Count for her husband: he must marry her under protest. In return for the trap she set him, he makes an ugly condition of his own: he will not accept her as wife before she gets a ring from his finger and bears him a child—seemingly impossible since he promptly leaves the country. Even granted the provocation, is this any way to treat a wife? Nothing daunted, she follows him in disguise and arranges to sleep with him in place of another girl he intends to seduce: she may be his wife, and therefore taking only what is hers by right, but is this any way to treat a husband? When she conceives the required child, she gives out that she is dead in order to bring her husband home. So he is outwitted, and, confronted by his wife in a suitably pregnant condition, he capitulates. The pair may be presumed to live uncomfortably ever after.

The emphasis in this tale is strongly on 'a woman's place', and *All's Well* is unusually rich in female parts and all-female scenes. W. W. Lawrence's argument in *Shakespeare's Problem Comedies* was that early folk-tales which tested female devotion assumed that there was virtue in a woman's single-mindedness. Shaw took a less historical view and found evidence of a very modern treatment of women in the story of Helena and her motives. In *Our Theatres in the Nineties* he not unexpectedly drew upon Ibsen for a comparison:

> Among Shakespeare's earlier plays, *All's Well That Ends Well* stands out artistically by the sovereign charm of the young Helena and the old Countess of Rousillon, and intellectually by the experiment, repeated nearly three hundred years later in *A Doll's House*, of making the hero a perfectly ordinary young man, whose unimaginative prejudices and selfish conventionality make him cut a very fine mean figure in the atmosphere created by the nobler nature of his wife. That is what gives a certain plausibility to the otherwise doubtful tradition that Shakespeare did not succeed in getting his play produced. (vol. I, p. 27)

Shaw had found a counterpart for Ibsen's *A Doll's House*, to which he was also drawn because of 'the ruin and havoc it made among the idols and temples of the idealists' (vol. III, p. 129). Kenneth Muir resists this in part when in *Shakespeare's Sources* he points out that 'the way Helena releases the King from his promise, her quiet submissiveness when Bertram repudiates her, and her wish to save him from the dangers of war all prevent us from feeling that she is merely a Shavian heroine who hunts down her prey' (p. 101). Nevertheless, it is hard to shake off the idea, once proposed, of a certain correspondence between the Nora / Helmer and the Helena / Bertram relationships.

The role of woman in society is impossible to consider without reference to that of the man, and the role of the wife must be understood by reference to the role of the husband. The double standard, which implies one law for the female and another for the male, is certainly a post-Ibsen concept, but its implications have existed from the beginning. If, as G. Wilson Knight suggests in *The Sovereign Flower*, honour between the sexes is at the heart of this play, with Helena a 'supreme expression of a woman's love, a humble medium for the divine power' (p. 106), she and Bertram will define such honour. The conventions of behaviour between the sexes display a duality by which men may flout their marriage vows, especially in the name of soldiering, while women must condone their conduct even as it diminishes them. Honour among Elizabethan men is, as Wilson Knight argues, martial; for the women it implies chastity and can never evade the strictures of female propriety. But when Bertram rushes off to the war to save his honour, it seems more as if he does it to save his face.

The so-called 'bed-trick', which here derives from Boccaccio and is used in many Elizabethan plays, raises the issues of the double standard most effectively on the stage. The idea of substituting one woman for another in bed in order to deceive the man may reduce the degree of modern psychological realism established in the characterisation, but in the context of comedy it did not necessarily raise moral eyebrows. In his introduction to his *New Arden* edition of the play, G. K. Hunter goes so far as to say,

> There was little sense among Shakespeare's contemporaries that this was a degrading and unsatisfactory way of getting a husband, either in real life or on the stage. No doubt an age which saw matrimony as a matter of social convenience rather than personal

> emotion accepted such means of obtaining a husband or wife as a
> smaller violation of the spirit of marriage than we can today.
> (p. xliv)

At all events, the bed-trick may at least be seen as a theatrical
way of pointing up the male and female roles within the world of
the play, and the fact that it works well for comedy need not
lessen the importance and interest of the problem of the double
standard in the real world of the audience.

The relationship of the sexes is of wide social interest, and yet
in life it is finally a personal matter. Drama is ideally suited to
explore the relationship, dealing as it must with general issues in
terms of the peculiar behaviour of individuals, and in *All's Well*
the distinctions between the male and female role emerge
sharply in the realistic mixture of motives found in Helena and
Bertram. In this play Shakespeare no more chose to stereotype
his principals than he did Troilus and Cressida or Antony and
Cleopatra. But if Helena represents the female principle, she
also displays an individual subtlety of mind and feeling that can
hardly represent all women. It may be that she is, in Milton
Shulman's view in *The Evening Standard* after watching Noël
Willman's production in 1955, 'the most ruthless single-minded
man-hunter in Shakespeare', but the playwright works to
confuse Helena's severest critics. Shulman went on to express
the contradiction thus: 'Having created a heroine with the brash
moral standards of an ambitious strumpet, Shakespeare proceeds to belie this interpretation in the dialogue. The incongruity
between what Helen does and what she says could not be
matched by the most cynical politician at election time' (27
April).

Shakespeare also chose to make Helena poor and low-born,
and so *All's Well* is also about the snobbery of one's station in
life, a subject only slightly less prickly. It is one designed to
emphasise the problems that Helena faces. Yet although the
differences in social rank between Helena and Bertram raise
barriers between them, her poverty and birth paradoxically
enable the play to speculate on the nature of her virtue indepen-
dently of class. This aspect of the play attracted William Poel in
1920 when he directed it in one of his 'vocal recitals' in the
Ethical Church, Bayswater. In *William Poel and the Elizabethan
Revival*, Robert Speaight reported of Poel that 'Just as he had

detected a plea for pacificism in *Troilus and Cressida*, so in *All's Well* he saw a plea for the removal of class barriers where the affections between men and women were in question' (p. 233). The presence of a restrictive social code which inhibited the expression of love not only appealed to Poel as a cause, but the modernity of the idea seemed to cry out for expression on the post-Ibsen stage. When Nunn set his production in the Edwardian period, he was able to affirm the play's sharp distinctions of class: Helena wore the house keys at her waist while Bertram spent time at the officers' club in Paris. The theme of class was arguably not essential to the play, but it in part explained the unmannerly behaviour of Bertram, and added a fine cutting edge to the image of Helena.

A third, perhaps more subtle, thread runs through the play, and also serves to accentuate the social issues in both individual and general terms. Shaw had remarked on the presence in the play of 'the most beautiful old woman's part ever written', that of the Countess of Rousillon. In performance it is apparent that the youth of the leading characters, Helena, Bertram, Diana and Parolles, is in each case precisely balanced by the greater age of their counterparts, the Countess, the King of France, the Widow of Florence and the old counsellor Lafeu. This distinctive and unusual patterning was early observed by A. W. Schlegel in his *Lectures on Dramatic Art and Literature* (1808), although he had not seen the play on the stage. In performance the differences in age are vivid and provocative, and have the effect of inviting every member of the audience, whatever his or her age, to see the situation from the alternating perspectives now of youth, now of age, so fashioning a more complete human experience, and adding considerably to the piquancy of the action. The young protagonists of the play learn their lessons by hard experience, while the audience is repeatedly granted an objective view of their thoughts and actions. If Shakespeare makes old age somewhat too reverend for its realistic context, so that it seems too gracious beside the general boorishness of the young as they suffer 'the staggers and the careless lapse / Of youth and ignorance' (II.3.161-2), it helps us recognise that young Helena may be able to cure the old King without being able so readily to cure Bertram and herself. Similarly, young Bertram may be a loyal son and faithful subject without knowing how to be a good husband.

The spectrum of a character: Helena

Now that *All's Well* is being performed more frequently, we are beginning to recognise the range of possible responses to it. The outrageous situation that Shakespeare creates for Helena and Bertram can be seen as cynically amusing or on the edge of tragedy, and today's actors and directors are legitimately searching out those points of dramatic power and interest with which they can reach their audience. Yet if the situation in the play continues unpredictable in its impact, so it is also with the characters. When a character has been committed to paper, it is not a finished creature, since the lines are only the occasion for the actor's interpretation. The text places limitations on his or her work, but it also provides for a spectrum of possibilities for performance, and while the actor may be faithful to the words, what is perceived in the theatre as the 'character' will be variable. Certainly, to judge from the Helenas seen in this century, her role is far from defined.

In the eighteenth century, Helena was played and seen as virtuous and long-suffering. In his *Dramatic Miscellanies* of 1783, Thomas Davies found that 'the passion of this sweet girl is of the noblest kind' (vol. II, p. 27). In this vein, it was possibly John Philip Kemble's revival of the play at Drury Lane in 1794 that prompted Coleridge to pronounce her Shakespeare's 'loveliest character'. The famous dictum on Helena in this period is Hazlitt's in his *Characters of Shakespeare's Plays* of 1818: 'The character of Helena is one of great sweetness and delicacy ... the most scrupulous nicety of female modesty is not once violated. There is not one thought or action that ought to bring a blush into her cheeks, or that for a moment lessens her in our esteem' (1920 edn., pp. 177-8). In our own time Wilson Knight in *The Sovereign Flower* has been the strongest advocate of this view, and sees Helena as 'loving, humble and good', 'the supreme development of Shakespeare's conception of human love' (p. 131). Knight goes on to assert that 'love such as Helena's is, at its best, a great aspiration, and yet one born of humility; in her, pride and humility are unified' (p. 139), and this becomes part of the proposition that she is a divine representative, working miracles by heavenly inspiration, so that 'religious values ... cluster round her as the values of war cluster round Bertram' (p. 144).

In this century, some still lean towards the pathos in the part. Benthall's sweetly yearning and impulsively innocent Claire Bloom was a conventionally simple heroine of romantic comedy 'who never stops to think of the ethical implications of things', according to *The Times* (16 September 1953). Harold Hobson in *The Sunday Times* thought she wore 'a look of childlike innocence, a clear and unashamed gaze', and by J. C. Trewin in *The Observer* was consequently dubbed 'like the play, a problem child' (both 20 September). Zoe Caldwell also escaped censure for her cunning by exuding simplicity and innocence, and her decision to heal the King and chase her husband clearly arose from the depth of her love for Bertram. Also sympathetic, Irene Worth's request for Bertram as a husband seemed mature, reasonable and even endearing; such honesty could give no offence. Benson's Helena, Florence Glossop-Harris, aimed at saintliness, and Nancy Wickwire under John Houseman's direction played her with a tragic seriousness: prompted by the speech in which she acknowledges the help of heaven, 'Of heaven, not me, make an experiment' (II.1.153), she became a providential Helena, descending a staircase slowly and quietly as if an angel had been sent from above.

However, the ambiguities in Helena's character have also been explored more fully. Her grief and her shyness can still be present, but so also are her wit and determination. The banter with Parolles about virginity is nowadays restored to its rightful place between the two moving soliloquies, 'O, were that all! I think not on my father' (I.1.73) and 'Our remedies oft in ourselves do lie' (I.1.202), and today we sense the balance of realism and romanticism in her character and acknowledge the mixture of criticism and sympathy in our reactions to her. Some part of the image of a grave and gentle heroine must persist: Mary Coleridge felt that 'she may be reckoned as one of the few women who have ever proposed for men and yet kept their charm' (quoted by George Gordon in *Shakespearian Comedy*, p. 30), and Kenneth Muir believes that she 'never loses our sympathy, especially when the play is performed' (*Shakespeare's Sources*, p. 101); but Helena's less ethereal, practical side, her comic aspect, has provoked a more interesting portrait.

Some early Helenas aimed at ambiguity. She appears to be a poor judge of men—the world of the court and the army are quite alien to her, a doctor's daughter. In *Shakespeare's Problem*

Plays, E. M. W. Tillyard also paired her with Parolles as an adventurer (p. 106), and in her essay, 'Virtue Is the True Nobility', M. C. Bradbrook thought of her as a 'social climber', so that she can also embody something of the designing female and the unscrupulous opportunist. Robert Atkins's first Helena, Jane Bacon, bravely rejected popularity and appeared to be more of a 'raffish, scheming, and hypocritical adventuress' (*The Sunday Times*, 4 December 1921), a girl who seemed to be mourning for her father when she was using the occasion only to supply a mask of grief for her love of Bertram. This Helena was a chameleon who could be merry with Parolles, shy with the Countess and confident with the King. Bridges-Adams's very pretty Helena, Maureen Shaw—slender, graceful and with masses of dark auburn hair, a figure who might have stepped out of a painting by Rossetti—solved the problem of being two-faced by assuming a charming girlishness, even if the charm was achieved at the expense of womanliness. In *Going to Shakespeare*, J. C. Trewin reported Bridges-Adams as saying, 'Molly was the prettiest thing in the world with an elfin wisdom; you forgave her everything' (p. 185). Payne's lovely Jean Shepeard, though a more modest Helena, also leaned towards youthfulness, and in the words of *The Daily Mail* presented the image of 'a disturbing and disturbed young blue-stocking' (24 April 1935). In this comic view of the part, we may have come closer to the Elizabethan idea of love as a mixture of courtly feelings and physical sickness awaiting cure, so described by Lawrence Babb in *The Elizabethan Malady*, p. 154.

Recently we have seen a more businesslike Helena, a study in practical feminine wiles with or without an accompanying charm. In 1955 Joyce Redman played her like a Victorian miss just out of finishing school, hiding her ruthlessness behind coy smiles and adopting the playfulness of a kitten. The effect of this was so disagreeable that the audience could not help but feel that she and Bertram deserved each other. In 1967 Estelle Kohler endowed Helena with a 'little girl' voice and, dressed in pale primrose, gave us a frighteningly clear-headed, slightly wicked, schoolgirl with an eye to the main chance. B. A. Young of *The Financial Times* decided that she was 'an ordinary inconsistent person' who knew quite well that she was playing a dirty trick on Bertram. This Helena turned the whole play round and established a realistic basis for the action. In *The Evening*

Standard Milton Shulman wrote, 'Behind those wide-open, round eyes and that perky-pretty face one can almost hear the ticking of a mind cunningly coiled into an efficient man-trap. It's quite clear that Bertram never had a chance.' Alan Brien capped this in *The Daily Telegraph:* 'Estelle Kohler plays her as a very young, mop-haired tomboy with gob stopper eyes and a crooked grin who enjoys teasing the King, cracking dirty jokes with Parolles, rehearsing charades with other girls, dressing up as a pilgrim and spoiling her runaway husband's dirty weekend in Florence' (all 2 June 1967).

It may be that the haunting performance of the American actress Martha Henry, in David Jones's Canadian production of 1977, has most precisely struck the balance between selfless wife and predatory female. It was a performance of restless high spirits and earnest feeling, and as a result of it John Fraser of *The Toronto Globe and Mail* pronounced Helena to be one of Shakespeare's most captivating characters, describing her as

> bluntly forward and loving in her manner, with a spirituality and grace left largely to any actress who dares take her on to define. . . . Helena is a complete woman who knows her own mind and pursues her own ambition. That her love for Bertram is not reciprocated is both a challenge to her constancy and a test for her vision . . . A woman, sure of her mind and her body—even today or perhaps especially today—who is in touch with both wonder and alienation. By evoking this and transmitting it through a loving nature, this great actress accomplished something profound and unique. (9 June)

When the Countess discovers that Helena loves her son, she says to her, 'Now I see / The myst'ry of your loneliness' (I.3.161-2), and this line delicately touched the source of life in the character as Martha Henry presented it.

The tendency towards revealing a more realistic Helena continued with the 'serenely unstoppable' Angela Down (the phrase is Jeremy Treglown's in *The Times Literary Supplement*, 9 January 1981) for the BBC TV production, a very mature and sober Helena. Miss Down came to a very human understanding of the contradictions in Helena's character. Everyone speaks of her honesty, while at the same time she appears to be an opportunist, and in the introduction to the BBC edition of the play, Henry Fenwick reported Miss Down as saying,

In Act III scene 2 she says, 'Oh, what have I done, isn't it awful? Now he's going off, possibly to get killed, and it's because of me, so the best thing I can do is leave so he can come home.' But the next thing she does is go to Florence—the very place where he is. She doesn't go to Alaska or Scotland or anywhere out of reach; she doesn't absent herself from the scene entirely, she gets right back into the heart of where the action is, so you think: 'Well, that's a funny place to go if what you want to do is get out of his hair!' But you often find in life, don't you, that you're saying and *meaning* one thing—and you do really mean it—but you find that you're *doing* something that is facilitating an event which might turn the tables. You think: 'Well, I won't actually tell him who I am, perhaps I'll just go and be near him' or whatever. But it so happens that in Florence she meets up with another opportunity that she then takes full advantage of. I think that's what I mean when I say she's an opportunist—not necessarily in a derogatory way. I simply mean that she puts herself in the way of opportunities and then when they arrive she takes full advantage of them. Nothing wrong with that! But it isn't by any means just a total innocent abroad! (p. 20)

The character grows richer as the part is filled out. It now seems important that in performance she should not only demonstrate a will of her own, but also be fired by some genuine sexual need, so that the audience may feel a maximum of tension in the character and her situation. Yet it is also essential she should retain her femininity, and even her maidenly modesty. For the force of her character, and indeed that of the whole play, lies in the very ambiguities and contradictions that make up the 'mingled yarn' of its life and challenge its audience.

The trouble with Bertram

The initial strength of Bertram's uncompromising character is one of the problems of this problem comedy. It has been hard for playgoers and critics not to think of him as a cad and a bounder, if not a snob and a prig, a cheat and a liar, and a boor and a coward. In spite of the blessing of his match with Helena by the King and the Countess themselves, Bertram's vanity quite blinds him to her finer points. So he begins by insulting and deserting his wife, goes on to play a rotten trick on his best friend, and ends by slandering the girl (Diana) who resisted his advances. For audiences, he has proved to be as big a source of disaffection with the play as Helena herself, and Samuel Johnson's early judgement sums the matter up as well as any:

> I cannot reconcile my heart to Bertram; a man noble without generosity, and young without truth; who marries Helen as a coward, and leaves her as a profligate; when she is dead by his unkindness, sneaks home to a second marriage, is accused by a woman whom he has wronged, defends himself by falsehood, and is dismissed to happiness. (*The Yale Edition of the Works of Samuel Johnson*, vol. VII, p. 404)

Shakespeare has sharply defined the role and carefully blackened his character, and we must accept this as a premise of the play. Some years ago in *Shakespeare Quarterly*, X.1, Francis Shoff wrote, 'It is not until we say, "No decent man could do to a girl what Bertram does to Helena and tries to do to Diana", that we run into trouble. In *All's Well* a decent man can and does' (p. 19).

It is true also that Bertram is a relatively unshaded, uncomplicated, character beside Helena, playing second fiddle to the heroine as Orlando does in *As You Like It*, but in the male/female relationship upon which the interest of the play is built, he must reflect some of her colour, and be the source of light in her. The chief quality the actor must justify in performance is Bertram's huge and unfeeling indifference to her, so that his rejection of his new wife must seem defensible. So, too, from the beginning he must disclose some of the reasons why Helena should love him enough to choose him for a husband, and, folk-tales notwithstanding, in the end he must find a sensible reason for the repentance which will bless their future together. Otherwise, she will seem to waste herself on him.

Helena admired Bertram's 'arched brows, his hawking eye, his curls' (I.1.88), and on the physical level an actor's good looks and dashing figure can to some degree justify an infatuation with him: W. A. Darlington observed of Ian Richardson's performance of Bertram as a wild young spark that he was very attractive to women, 'the kind that women want to marry aginst their better judgment' (*The Daily Telegraph*, 2 June 1967). The Countess thinks of her son as 'an unseason'd courtier' (I.1.64), and his youthfulness may also go some way towards explaining and compensating for his moral defects. If he is played as a young gallant who is a little green, his behaviour can smack of youthful vanity, and his profligacy can seem to be a forgivable slip rather than an ingrained vice. Certainly Bertram's youth would excuse his unwillingness to become a bridegroom at command, and the limited circle he moves in, that of Rousillon, the French court and the army, could explain some of the shock he receives when Helena traps him. Coleridge had no difficulty, it seems, in accepting him as a wayward young aristocrat: 'He was a young nobleman in feudal times, just bursting into manhood, with all the feelings of pride of birth and appetite for pleasure and liberty natural to such a character so circumstanced' (*Coleridge's Shakespearean Criticism*, p. 356). And in his essay on 'The Structure of *All's Well That Ends Well*', S. Nagarajan has summed up the case for Bertram's immaturity: 'It palliates his rejection of Helen, explains his trust in Parolles and softens the enormity of his affair with Diana,' as well as giving 'a dramatic significance to his wardship' (p. 24). Guthrie's audiences accordingly saw him very much as a boy, with Edward de Souza playing him in 1959 as 'a stuffy, dirty-minded schoolboy', according to *The Spectator* of 24 April.

However, a balance of approval and disapproval of Bertram is not easily achieved, and may not even be desirable. If he is played for sympathy, as he was when Raymond Raikes played him in 1935, Helena runs the risk of seeming less pure. It has been more usual for him to seem remote, as he was in Benthall's production, in which John Neville was merely Claire Bloom's unattainable Prince Charming. In 1922, Maurice Colbourne was positively Byronic in his noble pride and scorn, and struck attitudes on every occasion, so that Helena's virtues shone more brightly and Bertram seemed insufferable in his patronising, 'a pure jackanapes' who left the critic of *The Daily Telegraph* 'speechless with rage' (25 April). In 1981, Mike Gwilym's Bertram was 'a savage Strindbergian monster' (Michael Billington).

Some degree of realistic motivation for Bertram has occasionally been attempted. Ian Richardson, playing for John Barton with an icy correctness of demeanour, presented a very proper young nobleman whose resentment at being forced into marriage was perfectly understandable. Guthrie's Canadian Bertram, Donald Harron, was a young fool. He had grown up in a household dominated by women and consequently idolised someone of his own sex, Parolles. When Bertram found himself tricked into marriage, he naturally turned to Parolles for consolation. But this Bertram grew up, and when he was disillusioned with his friend, he was ready for a girl of his own choice. In *Renown at Stratford*, Robertson Davies commented, 'At last, when he is ready for the kind of woman that Helena is, Helena is waiting for him. It needs no psychoanalyst, surely, to understand this entirely normal pattern of a young man's development?' (p. 75). The Bertram who grew up was lucky, of course, to find himself still loved by a woman of unusual understanding.

The question remains whether the ugly side of Bertram's character should be obscured. A. P. Rossiter pointed out in *Angel with Horns* that Bertram's lack of heroic qualities is characteristic of the problem comedies, arguing that in this part 'Shakespeare produced something more psychologically plausible, more complicated—and disagreeable', for *All's Well* was not to be a fairy tale of Beauty and the Beast (p. 88). The final scene of the play is perhaps the test.

Bertram's problems as a character come to a head in the last scene, when he must convince the audience that his contempt for his wife has finally turned to love. Shakespeare delays the reunion of the two to some purpose, and Diana stage-manages an expert *coup de théâtre* by concealing the truth that Helena is still alive for as long as possible. In the realistic perspective on the play, it is again a question of balance: since Bertram behaved badly at court, the trick played on him must fit the crime; since he taunted Helena with her poverty, he must be taunted no less with his irresponsibility. His blustering and his disclaimers of the last act must shame and ridicule him for his former pride, and if the audience wanted to kick him in the first half of the play, the last act does it for them. The doubts about Bertram felt by the audience finally need the satisfaction of seeing him treated as harshly as possible.

Youth and age

In *All's Well* the young tend to disregard their elders, and in his 1967 production John Barton actually based the theme of his programme notes on the idea that 'crabbed age and youth cannot live together'. A glance at the *dramatis personae* of the play will show that distinctions of age are explicit: among the principals four are young and four are old, and Elijah Moshinsky had even the Countess's steward Rinaldo played as an old man. In performance, the differences in age clarify for the audience its questioning of what is proper or improper behaviour: we are urged to distinguish between experience and inexperience, between wisdom and folly, and modify our judgements accordingly.

David Jones's production at Stratford, Ontario in 1977 emphasised the contrast strongly. Richard Eder reported in *The New York Times* that the play was directed 'without flamboyance and with an acute sense of where the play's real strength lies. It is not in the young people, despite all their activity, but in the old ones.' For Rousillon, Tanya Moiseiwitsch designed an autumnal scene, and the clown Lavache opened the play like a gardener, 'sweeping dead leaves away from a sundial. He chews on a green leaf. Time is the setting for the appearance of the Countess.' And as the Countess, Margaret Tyzack especially helped to place the emphasis on gracious age. She had lived through her own years of passion, and although at first Helena's love for her son seemed unthinkable, 'she sees that new life must replenish old power, and she embraces her daughter-in-law long before her son does' (9 June). When the King directed Bertram to abandon his social prejudices, he and the Countess appeared to be more liberal than the young, so that, as the play proceeded, the Countess seemed to grow young herself, and the autumnal years hung lightly on her person.

The Countess of Rousillon is the maternal *grande dame* of the play's events and Helena's fortunes, the still centre which gives the audience faith that all will yet be well. This gracious part has never failed any actress in the distinguished line of those who have played her in recent times: Catherine Lacey, Eleanor Stuart, Fay Compton, Rosalind Atkinson, Edith Evans, Margaret Tyzack, Celia Johnson, Peggy Ashcroft. Together with Lafeu and Lavache in this play, she was wholly of Shakespeare's own invention.

Her dominant trait is one of charm and compassion, although her gravity has on occasion seemed at odds with the activities of the younger set. Alan Brien in *The Spectator* thought that Edith Evans looked like 'an exiled queen locked away in a madhouse' (24 April 1959) because of the un-Elizabethan surprises of Guthrie's production. But her quiet role need not necessarily be monotonous: when she persuades Helena to confess her love for her son (I.3), and when she condemns Bertram for scorning Helena (III.2), the Countess also betrays a sharp, autocratic temper. Peggy Ashcroft added a sense of humour: when Helena announced that she was going to Paris to cure the King, she raised her eyebrows for 'This was your motive for Paris, was it, speak?' Even when the Countess sometimes seems composed in her demeanour, she must also feel the stress of loving both her unworthy son and the forsaken Helena at the same time, for she is mother to both.

The King of France is no less compassionate, a father to the orphaned Helena. His part, however, is less rewarding, since he is confined by his sickness for some of the play and stereotyped by his throne for the rest. The sternly judgemental bent of his scenes has nevertheless in practice admitted a few variations that have extended the role.

For television, Donald Sinden played him fiercely, a man dying an angry death. When Helena comes to cure him in II.1, Lafeu's little joke about being 'Cressid's uncle' suggested that a man suffering from a fistula may also be playfully aware of her sex, and encouraged Sinden to play the King like an old lecher on his deathbed. However, Jeremy Treglown in *The Times Literary Supplement* deplored the overt introduction of sex into a scene which he thought should carry only spiritual overtones: 'His miraculous cure, in this interpretation, looks as if it will involve Helena in some kind of health-farm sauna activities—a plan she seems to go along with, kissing the repellent old satyr compliantly at the end of a gropy II.1 which both goes against her performance of the character otherwise and steals attention for the hammy Sinden' (9 January 1981). For the defence, Stanley Kauffmann in *The Dial* considered that 'it becomes clear that Helena's womanliness is having as much effect on the monarch as her promise of a cure. With no scintilla of vulgarity, Down and Sinden tell us that the King is regaining vigour because of his response to *her*, and the scene ends with a gentle kiss. Thus the action buried within the lines sustains the scene' (June 1981, p. 10).

When the King has been cured, Shakespeare evidently intends him to prove it by showing that he is 'able to lead her a coranto' (II.3.40). This is an arresting moment on the stage, as Guthrie demonstrated when Alec Guiness came waltzing in with Irene

Worth in his arms. He had substituted a waltz for a coranto, of course, but the key to the effect lies in the Elizabethan coranto itself, as lively a dance as Shakespeare could command, with its 3/4 time, its running and jumping steps, and the balancing and bowing: all to persuade us that the King is not only cured, but positively rejuvenated. When Bertram thwarts him in this scene, the King's new strength and anger are unmistakable: 'My honour's at the stake' (line 149). Laurence Hardy played the part as a buffoon who expected his court to laugh at all his jokes, so undermining the importance of the injunctions upon Bertram and Helena: in his essay 'Plays Pleasant and Plays Unpleasant' for *Shakespeare Survey* 8, Richard David reported that on his sickbed Hardy 'was attended by a couple of comic doctors, one fat, one thin, and by a friar who kept up a running Paternoster in a high monotone. His speeches were punctuated by sudden grimaces and yowling cries as his ailment griped him' (p. 134). This King of France could not strike the sobering note of his speech on honour, nor establish the contrast between wisdom and folly designed to prompt our sense of the outrageous in what Bertram and Helena then proceed to do.

The Folio of 1623 has 'old' Lafeu, and after Rowe designated him 'an old lord', he has been an elderly courtier ever since. He is a rather caustic counsellor, but everybody's confidant, a wise old man who may be comic to a degree, but no fool. Rupert Harvey was honest and blunt for Robert Atkins in 1921, and when Atkins came to play him himself in 1940, he was 'a kind of grave Sir Toby'. When played by William Squire for Benthall in 1953, he was 'an amiable pippin', and Guthrie's Michael Bates in Canada and Anthony Nicholls in England played him as an aristocrat with a salty tongue, able to make jokes with the ladies that only his rank and age could allow. On television Michael Hordern introduced a melancholy note that suited the sober quality of Moshinsky's production. But Lafeu has wit enough to enjoy the wit in Parolles, and wisdom enough to show him mercy at the end.

Lavache presents more of a problem. 'Feste's wry smile has turned to a leer in Lavache', writes Robert Goldsmith in *Wise Fools in Shakespeare* (p. 58). He enjoys more bawdy than any other clown in Shakespeare; he shares with Touchstone of *As You Like It* his realistic attitude to marriage, and his relationship with Isbel ('I am driven by the flesh; and he must needs go that the devil drives', I.3.28) echoes Touchstone's with Audrey ('As the ox hath his bow, sir, the horse his curb, and the falcon her bells, so man hath his desires; and as pigeons bill, so wedlock would be nibbling', *As You Like It*, III.3.69); but in his need to satisfy his drives, Lavache is an unhappy man.

He is the ageless clown turned sour, but he remains the company's funny man whose humour, like Touchstone's, must reside as much in the actor as in his lines. Payne's Kenneth Wicksteed succeeded in milking them for laughs, although he failed to please the correspondent of *The Birmingham Mail*, who found his wit out-of-date and pointless to the modern ear (24 April 1935). But is he the rustic clown like old Gobbo, or is he a dry and rather cynical chorus figure like Thersites? Production has inclined towards the latter. The part has regularly distressed critics and reviewers because of the coarseness of his dialogue with the Countess, and, as played by Edward Atienza as a hunchbacked dwarf in 1955, or as Geoffrey Hutchings's hunch-backed comedian in a bowler hat flirting with all the ladies (1981), he can add a disturbing note which would darken the darkest of dark comedies. A misanthropic Paul Brooke played him mirthlessly for television, and Guthrie simply left him out.

From his source material in Painter's *The Palace of Pleasure* Shakespeare carved out a single character from Helena's hostess in Florence and the mother of Diana. The Widow of Florence is a surrogate for the Countess in foreign parts, standing up nobly for the two girls, Diana and Helena. Her daughter Diana is described by one of the French lords as 'a young gentlewoman ... of a most chaste renown' (IV.3.13-14), and she has chiefly been played as a virtuous maiden in a difficult predicament, the innocent object of Bertram's attentions. But Bertram pronounced her to be 'a common gamester to the camp' (V.3.186), and this slander has encouraged another interpretation. Beginning with Payne's Rosamund Merivale in 1935, she has also been played as an impudent minx, a jolly girl full of the tricks sometimes prompted by her mother. Nunn went so far as to have Cheryl Campbell sing a café song like Piaf, which Stanley Wells considered to have diminished her: 'the role loses some of the symbolical aspects hinted at in the name. It is not impossible that an attractive girl who sings seductive songs, dances and shows her petticoats to soldiers in a café should take pride in her chastity, but it is difficult to believe that she should be 'of a most chaste renown in the camp' (*The Times Literary Supplement*, 27 November 1981). In 'Dramatic Emphasis in *All's Well*', Harold Wilson considers her, indeed, to be Helena's *alter ego*, intended to show the audience what Helena might have been.

In characterising the Widow and her daughter, Guthrie saw the need of few restrictions. Having seen the Canadian production, Robertson Davies argued in *Renown at Stratford*,

> The social distinctions of the Renaissance are not familiar to us, and even distinctions indicated by costume may escape us . . . But in a modern dress production we have no trouble at all in placing the characters. We see in what ways this Florentine Widow differs from the Countess of Rousillon; the difference is approximately that between a woman who looks forward to the Old Age Pension, and one who must make provision against the Death Duties. And when Diana at last appears at court, in her charming frock, we can see at a glance how this frock differs from the gowns of the ladies to whom court is an accustomed place. (p. 94)

So in Canada Amelia Hall and Beatrice Lennard assumed strong Northern Ontario accents and became the keepers of a Canadian Tourist Home, specialising in pilgrims bound for the shrine of St Jacques le Grand. They were ladies of good family but reduced circumstances, so that, however good a girl Diana might be, she would be sufficiently flattered by the attentions of an army officer.

Guthrie continued to be attracted to the idea of the inferior class of the Widow and Diana. In England he went a step further, and in *The Spectator* Alan Brien reported that Priscilla Morgan played Diana as 'a wartime factory tart who sits on the doorstep in nightgown and housecoat, with a turban on her head and a lollipop in her mouth, giggling the lines in coffee-bar Cockney'. As her mother, Angela Baddeley was 'an old bag of tricks from a Giles cartoon swathed in a purple knitted dress, strangled in Woolworth beads, and choking over her nightcap of gin' (24 April 1959). That production evidently did not see the Widow as an extension of the Countess, and certainly not a further embodiment of 'aged honour'.

Elijah Moshinsky could not accept this treatment of the Widow when he cast Rosemary Leach for the part in the television production. In the introduction to the BBC edition of the play, Henry Fenwick records the director's decision:

> 'I didn't want a comedy actress to do a cameo,' Moshinsky says.

'What would Helena learn from a comedy turn? I wanted the Widow to be someone Helena would learn from.' Rosemary Leach's Widow, a fully-rounded character fleshed out from the hints in the text, is a rather gossipy, perhaps slightly flighty woman, frightened by the precariousness of her position, but fundamentally honest, tough and no one's fool. The character has become a very strong presence. (p. 18)

Parolles and his plot

Shakespeare also added Parolles (usually pronounced with three syllables (*paro'lis*) in order to regularise the iambic verse line) and his story to Painter's original, and an extraordinary amount of the play is given over to him, the scenes which ridicule him falling largely in the second half: the loss of the drum (III.6), the ambush (IV.1) and the interrogation (IV.3).

This emphasis on Parolles may account for the curious detail of history that for many years the success of *All's Well* on the stage depended on his performance. He was the braggart of ancient and popular tradition, a man who is all word and no deeds, and something of a fop as well ('The soul of this man is his clothes', says Lafeu in his ready wisdom, II.5.43). History records that a succession of notable comedians, Joseph Peterson, Theophilus Cibber (son of Colley Cibber) and Charles Macklin, helped the play through the early eighteenth century. In his *Letters* William Shenstone describes how a swaggering Cibber played him in 1742 as a 'shabby gentleman' and a 'bully character' in a rusty black coat and gloves, adding 'and a face!—which causes five minutes laughter' (ed. Marjorie Williams, p. 42). Then in 1756 Garrick arranged the text to make sure that Parolles was right at the centre of the play, and put the comedian Henry Woodward at the top of the bill at Drury Lane: 'Capt. Parolles by Mr Woodward'.

For many years, therefore, Parolles overshadowed the story of Helena and Bertram, and as late as 1935 he could steal the show in Payne's production, as played by the massive Falstaffian figure of Roy Emerton. Nevertheless, he had faded in importance in the previous century. In 1793 John Philip Kemble had cut back his scenes, and at Covent Garden in 1811 John Fawcett was hissed in the part: the comedy was missing. In 1852 Phelps played him briefly at Sadler's Wells without success, in spite of the popularity of this actor. And in this century Parolles has often had to struggle to find his rightful place in the play. Benson's performance in 1916 was considered to be artificial and forced because it depended on too much by-play. In *The New Age* John Francis Hope reported that Ernest Milton in the part in 1921 was 'like someone skating on very thin ice, as though he were trying to spare Helena's blushes instead of provoking them' (15 December).

These last instances may also indicate that the braggart part was losing its traditional force in the eyes of the public. The conventional thinking was that, as a soldier, he occupied a position between the Falstaff of *Henry IV* and the Pistol of *Henry V*, although traits from Dogberry, Sir Toby Belch and even Malvolio were recognised in him. Ernest Milton was surly and burly, 'a Falstaff with all the red blood taken out of his body' (*The Sunday Times*, 4 December 1921). The most famous in this line was Baliol Holloway, swaggering in cloak and gauntlets for Bridges-Adams in 1922. Holloway was a 'rough-cut gem', 'a mixture of Hindenburg [the ex-German Marshal] and Falstaff', 'a Pistol translated to higher society' (*The Birmingham Mail*, 24 April).

More recently, the characterisation of Parolles has been diversified and given a slightly more realistic treatment. In Barry Jackson's modern dress production of 1927 with the Birmingham Repertory Company, Laurence Olivier played him as a smart young man. Douglas Campbell, also prompted by more modern costuming, caught the exuberance of Guthrie's production of 1953, and wore his khaki battle-shorts with a flair. Walter Kerr in *The New York Herald Tribune* thought him 'a small masterpiece of comic dishonesty' who invented imaginary exploits on the field of battle 'with a sham reticence that is infinitely funny' (16 July). Cyril Luckham, playing the part in Guthrie's English production in 1959, however, seemed to Philip Hope-Wallace in *The Manchester Guardian* to be 'a fugitive from the Army Game' and more a caricature of 'a certain well-known bogus major type' (23 April). Muriel St Clare Byrne found this quite acceptable, and in *Shakespeare Quarterly* for that autumn decided that 'in our time he has again become a propper-up of bar counters ... He will always manage to eat at somebody's expense' (p. 562). At the Old Vic in 1953, Michael Hordern played him as a scruffily theatrical type trying to keep his dignity with Lafeu and 'tremendously man-of-the-world', according to J. C. Trewin in *The Observer*, a Parolles who found 'the right stab' for the lines which drop him from farce to reality, 'Who cannot be crush'd with a plot?' and 'Simply the thing I am / Shall make me live' (20 September). In an interview with Robert Speaight, reported in *Shakespeare Quarterly* for winter 1976, Jonathan Miller said that Parolles was 'the kind of young man whom the Countess wished her son would not bring back to the house' (p. 22), and consequently cast him in his Greenwich production of 1975 to be the same age as Bertram, disconcertingly dressing them both in identical Elizabethan costumes.

Whatever character Parolles adopts, however, there are two problems that confront him in performance. The first is his personal relationship with the principals, Helena and Bertram. If he plays an out-and-out villain, as in John Houseman's production, it is easy to see that he warms us towards them. He is hardly a good friend to either, but such simple stereotyping does not help the actor who must play him with any degree of conviction. He may survive the early 'virginity scene' with Helena, which shows him unsympathetically enough, but he must exercise a powerful influence over Bertram, for which the strongest clue is found in Lafeu's lines,

> No, no, no, your son was misled with a snipt-taffeta fellow there, whose villainous saffron would have made all the unbak'd and doughy youth of a nation in his colour. Your daughter-in-law had been alive at this hour, and your son here at home, more advanc'd by the King than by that red-tail'd humble-bee I speak of. (IV.5.1-6)

In performance the two men must be shown to be close friends who are very much in harmony with one another, but Benthall made Parolles wholly responsible for Bertram's behaviour, giving him his cue at every step by a nod or a beck, and even thwarting the parting kiss to Helena with whispered advice. Unless Parolles is afforded a degree of humanity, this treatment reduces the strength and integrity of Bertram's part and may make puppets of both of them.

The second problem concerns the trick played upon him by Bertram and his friends. How far is Parolles finally a figure of pathos, like Malvolio and Falstaff? The test comes when he has been teased to distraction and his blindfold at last taken off; he looks about him at the faces he knows so well and speaks the line, 'Who cannot be crush'd with a plot?' (IV.3.302), faintly echoing Malvolio's 'Madam, you have done me wrong, / Notorious wrong' (*Twelfth Night*, V.1.315-6). How those lines are spoken and received decides whether we feel contempt or sympathy. When he utters his next lines, 'Yet I am thankful. If my heart were great, / 'Twould burst at this' (307-8), he can be nearly as moving as the rejected Falstaff of *Henry IV, Part II*. Nevertheless, Parolles need not sink into absolute disgrace. In his essay, 'The Life of Shame: Parolles and *All's Well*', Robert Hapgood made an issue of Parolles's vitality, and criticised Michael Hordern's deflation of the Falstaffian line, 'Simply the thing I am / Shall make me live' (IV.3.310) by approving Charles Taylor's production at the Ashland, Oregon Festival in 1961, when Parolles delightfully vaulted to his feet to face the world again.

The question remains why Parolles is in the play at all. In his introduction to the new Cambridge edition, Quiller-Couch thought him 'about the inanest of all Shakespeare's creations', and that he could be 'cut out of the story, like a wen, without the smallest detriment to the remaining tissue' (p. xxiv). In *Shakespeare's Problem Comedies* W. W. Lawrence more circumspectly observed about the sub-plot that it was 'singularly independent of the main action; much more so than is usual with Shakespeare's mature work' (p. 33). The argument has even been advanced separately by Harold Wilson and Kenneth Muir that by placing so much emphasis on Parolles, Shakespeare was simply trying to obscure the unpleasantness of Helena's activities in the last two acts. But is Parolles merely introduced for 'comic relief', a foil to set off Helena's story?

In the *New Arden* introduction, G. K. Hunter offers a strong set of reasons why Bertram's story would not be the same without Parolles:

> There is a continual parody of the one by the other. Parolles and Helena are arranged on either side of Bertram, placed rather like the Good and Evil Angels in a Morality. His selfish ostentation balances her selfless abnegation; both are poor people making good in a world open to adventurers, but the magical and romantic actions of Helena are in strong contrast to the prosaic opportunism of Parolles—the contrast perhaps working both ways, staining the career of Helena with the imputation of ambition as well as showing up the degraded mind of Parolles.

Parolles wins (temporarily at least) the battle for Bertram's soul (it is he who ships him off to the war), and is himself an index to the world of lust and lies into which Bertram is falling. (p. xxxiii)

We would like to believe this, and after watching the Guthrie production of 1959, Muriel St Clare Byrne believed she saw how Parolles contributed to the balance and symmetry of the play, 'the music of the whole composition', as she called it, for Parolles not only helps to separate Helena and Bertram, he actually helps to bring them together: 'As go-between for Bertram and Diana, Parolles, in his ignorance, becomes the go-between for the wife and husband whom he has helped to separate, and the way for virgins to "undermine" men is discovered when the realism of consummating his own marriage, unawares, undermines Bertram's would-be romantic seduction of Diana' (p. 565).

The comedy of Parolles is more complicated than has commonly been supposed. It is successful because the role, a little like Falstaff's, exhibits many contrary masks. He is a choric philosopher, a stand-up comedian, the traditional comic coward and traitor, and, finally ostracised, a rather pathetic victim. Through the comedy of Parolles and his drum, soldiering is seen less gloriously, just as it is when Bertram, the off-duty officer, makes his attempt on the virtue of Diana. And when Parolles is cut down to size in the scene of his unmasking, he brings down with him the companion in arms who had shared his courtly world of false gallantry, the very man who had unmasked him, Bertram. Finally, in performance the presence of Parolles serves powerfully to juxtapose the careless activity in which he and Bertram sport themselves with our more thoughtful concern for the hard moral issues that surround Helena and all she represents.

PART II

Scene by scene

ACT I

I.1.1-92: Rousillon in mourning

The play begins with a gently melancholy, but businesslike, exposition, one rich in atmosphere and strong in suppressed feelings. It is a domestic scene, suggesting 'a room in the palace of Rousillon', as the old editors have it, possibly a room where Bertram's bags are being packed; but it can take place wherever the young Count may take leave of his mother, and the old Countess of her son: 'In delivering my son from me, I bury a second husband.' The Countess's first line reflects her sense of birth and death, beginning and ending.

To capture this mood is the first task. The sad occasion is visually darkened by the sombre clothes all are wearing in mourning for the death of the old Count. The Folio specifies 'all in black', and so the Countess's old counsellor Lafeu is also in black, along with any attendants. So, too, is Helena, simply and severely dressed, doubly in mourning for the Count and for her own father, the physician Gerard de Narbon. Shakespeare uses costume; the actors contribute voices and pace. Voices are low and slow, and the talk of death continues when Lafeu reports that the king of France is also dying and has given up hope: 'He

hath abandon'd his physicians, madam; under whose practices
he hath persecuted time with hope, and finds no other advantage
in the process but only the losing of hope by time.'

Thus there are four reasons to be sad, and the scene is heavily
nostalgic. To add to the effect, Willman had Lavache introduce
the scene with a soft guitar, his back to the audience. Jones had
him sweeping autumn leaves about a sundial, and Guthrie also
aimed at an autumnal mood, as Muriel St Clare Byrne
recounted:

> An elegaic sadness broods over the neglected garden of Rousillon.
> Brown, withered leaves and broken branches droop mournfully in
> a classic urn in a niche of the deserted summerhouse: there is the
> melancholy of autumn in the pale clear light. It is a moment of
> departure ... Life is ebbing away from the great house, leaving
> the women behind. It is prologue to the desolation of Helena's
> unattainable love, and to the shadow of mortality which hangs
> over the King's court. It is also the perfect dramatic contrast for
> setting off the upsurge of her ardent will and the vitality which
> nerves her to find remedy in action. (*Shakespeare Quarterly*, X.4,
> p. 558)

Nunn's production began with a melancholy waltz by Guy
Woolfenden to which the figures of Bertram and Helena circled
slowly in symbolic silhouette before the stage erupted with a
flurry of servants carrying Bertram's luggage and golf clubs.
Except for Helena, the players make a small group, standing
close together in their grief. To emphasise family intimacy in
another way, Payne had the traverse curtains of his inner stage
drawn back to 'discover' the Countess kissing Bertram in
tableau.

Only Helena, in the care of the Countess since her father died,
is not quite one of the family, and she does not speak. She stands
a little apart, delicately withdrawing herself and her eyes until
attention is given to her. The first reference to her presence,
'This young gentlewoman', had her drop to her knees in the
Bridges-Adams and Payne productions, suggesting her deference
and her inferiority, but Guthrie had her move slowly downstage
and across the front as the Countess and Lafeu spoke of her.
Reference to Helena's tears indicates that she is crying softly,
and the Countess moves to comfort her: 'No more of this, Helena,
go to.' On the suggestion that she is in love with her own grief,
Helena may make a nervous movement away, as she did for

Bridges-Adams, for she responds with a quibble that is almost an aside: 'I do affect a sorrow indeed, but I have it too.' Until she is alone, we are not fully to understand this puzzle. It will emerge that, by appearing to be grieving for her father, she is able both to conceal and to express her feelings about the departure of Bertram. Guthrie had her look at him on the line, more quickly dispelling the mystery.

The pattern of relationships is soon established, and with them the strong, simple pattern of the scene. First we see the warm embrace of the Countess and Bertram, with Helena the outsider looking askance at them from a position apart. She is isolated, revealing only her tearfulness, and perhaps a touch of envy. The television camera caught her in long shot, mere glimpses of her, first between the Countess and Lafeu, then between the mother and son. Second, we see that the positions are reversed, with the Countess embracing her 'other child' and comforting Helena, while Bertram in irritation moves apart (the Edwardian Bertrams Mike Gwilym and Philip Franks looked at their watches, impatient to leave) and is himself isolated for a moment. It is almost a sibling rivalry.

Through all this, the main focus is on Helena, but Bertram, the object of her attention, appears to ignore her in the text almost from start to finish. This was very pointed in Payne's production when Bertram wandered away upstage, pacing impatiently, as soon as Lafeu and the Countess began to talk of Helena again on, 'Was this gentlewoman the daughter of Gerard de Narbon?' And with a flush of anger Bertram may abruptly cut in by kneeling to his mother on, 'Madam, I desire your holy wishes.' When the Countess offers him some advice in a brisker verse, 'Love all, trust a few, / Do wrong to none', she seems already to make a comment on his behaviour. Then with a kiss to the head ('What heaven more will . . . Fall on thy head'), she raises him to his feet and embraces him again. Willman had her also give a dignified curtsy to the new Count, thus emphasising distinction in rank. Moshinsky had her give him a ring on the mention of 'thy birthright', the very ring which will play its part in the action to come. With that, the Countess leaves Bertram to Lafeu, going off through one exit, the men going off through another. The parting will be seen to be complete.

Helena is now made to feel her isolation. When Guthrie's Bertram spoke his parting words to his mother, 'The best wishes that can be forg'd in your thoughts be servants to you!', it was Helena he looked in the eye, patting her on the arm precisely on the word 'servants'. Thus was Helena put down visually. Even Lafeu's parting shot is jocular—'Farewell, pretty lady'—and on this line Guthrie had him pat her on the cheek. In performance Helena's costume is not enough to mark her difference in rank, and some such gesture of disrespect will make the point, as well as prepare us for the insulting conversation she is soon to have with Parolles.

In *The Unfortunate Comedy* Joseph Price considers that too premature a revelation of Bertram's personality destroys the dramatic effect of Helena's admission of her love:

> His 'Madam, I desire your holy wishes' may be a brash interruption in the discussion of grief, but even as such, it is no worse than might be expected from an 'unseason'd courtier'. In itself, the line is indifferent; the suggestion of a faulty text, the insertion of stage business, or merely the intonation of the voice obscures Shakespeare's intention. Indifferent too are his parting words to Helena, 'Be comfortable to my mother, your mistress, and make much of her.' But surely in this case, their indifference is the very point of the lines. There is neither warmth nor scorn. From Bertram's view, the departing son bids the household dependent to assist his mother. An indifferent Bertram intensifies the effect of Helena's soliloquy. (p. 139)

The point is well taken, but for an audience trying to recognise the relationships between the principals on stage at the beginning of the play, it must be a kindness to make Bertram's indifference more vivid, else the irony in Helena's soliloquy will be diminished. It is a question whether indifference can best be conveyed by indifference itself. Price goes on to say that Helena 'constantly follows Bertram on stage to interpret his conduct through her love', since 'the reaction of the audience is not to be fixed by his conduct; rather, the conduct is to be reconsidered in the light of her love' (p. 140). It would be fairer to say that the quality of her love is revealed by the conflict between his conduct and her response to it.

At Stratford, Ontario in 1953 Helena gazed longingly after Bertram as he and Lafeu took their long walk upstage; it may have been so on the platform of Shakespeare's Globe. The proscenium stage often leaves her looking off to one side less effectively. A simple point about her difference from the rest of the family has been made, and the scene shows her, now crying

[37]

more openly, a lonely figure on an empty stage. There is a terrible honesty about the thoughts she next expresses in soliloquy—she cannot mourn for her father because of her love for Bertram, and she connot recall her father's face because she cannot forget Bertram's:

> I have forgot him. My imagination
> Carries no favour in't but Bertram's.
> I am undone; there is no living, none,
> If Bertram be away.

Payne had her sit despondently on a stool downstage; Willman dropped the lights a little. Guthrie had her half run after Bertram, and then return to collapse on the stage beside a seat. Television had her play a melancholy air on a virginal, her face and head motionless in silhouette, her 'voice over' heard speaking in low tones. The convention of the soliloquy exposes her inner secrets while at the same time suggesting that, like Viola in *Twelfth Night* who must also suppress her love, she is living in a world of her own, knowing too well that Bertram 'is so above me'. When she says, 'The hind that would be mated by the lion, / Must die for love', despair is still heard in her voice, but there is also a new strength in the lines. She will possibly wipe her eyes and speak more steadily. Guthrie had her resolutely get up and sit on the seat. The emphasis is again on death, but now it is her own, and this is the first we see of the new Helena, the Helena whose tenacity will carry her through the challenges she will face in the rest of the play.

The play has begun nervously, and any prudish cutting at this stage, as in Bridges-Adams's production, must reduce the tension and damage our sense of Helena's keyed-up sexuality. If the pain of personal conflict is to be felt, it is important to recognise the restraints of her maidenliness; but her passions are ready to explode, and Guthrie was even able to suggest that she was emotionally on the rebound from the loss of her father too. In this opening Shakespeare calls for a most complicated heroine who can find no peace with herself, deeply torn as she is between her situation and her desire.

I.1.93-215: Virginity assailed

Before Helena speaks in soliloquy again, Shakespeare interposes a startling interview with Parolles. It is an episode whose subject and tone can radically change our image of Helena, her predicament and the play; it is a shift of perspective quite deliberately required. Yet of all the scenes in the play, this used to be thought of as a blot, and has been the most butchered. It does indeed constitute the dramatic equivalent of an assault on Helena's innocence and virtue, for it is one which thrusts her into the coarser world in which Bertram moves. In her introduction to the *New Penguin Shakespeare* text (p. 25), Barbara Everett even suggests that this scene drops the hint that Helena's only hope of gaining Bertram's love is to do it in the way he himself tries with Diana later. At all events, the exchange with Parolles that now follows prepares us for the worldliness of the people and events we are soon to meet, and also manages to remind us that Helena is not regarded as much more than a servant.

'Who comes here?' is the kind of line the Elizabethan theatre used when a character already on stage near the audience wished to draw the audience's attention to a new character making an upstage entrance. We see Parolles, wonderfully over-dressed in the uniform of an officer of the army of the King, strutting the distance down to Helena's side. As he comes, she conveniently describes him for us, and at the same time reveals that she knows him to be 'a notorious liar' and 'a great way fool, solely a coward'. Yet she will love him for Bertram's sake, and like Cressida with Pandarus, adopt his prosaic tone to hold her own with him. The modest maiden shows she also has wit:

> *Parolles.* Save you, fair queen.
> *Helena.* And you, monarch.
> *Parolles.* No.
> *Helena.* And no.

She curtsies ironically to him, but the point is that Parolles has hardly addressed her as a lady might expect. When Ernest Milton played Parolles diffidently (see p. 30) he made the moment a small triumph for the girl instead of making her aware of his vulgarity. When Barton's Parolles went so far as to put his arm round her waist on 'Are you meditating on virginity?', there was altogether more bite in the scene.

The shift from the romantic to the real, from Helena's meditations on her love to the caustic dialogue on her virginity, is not easy. She must show us two faces, one of the sorrowing girl and another of the spirited young woman. The abruptness of the transition was mitigated somewhat in Willman's production by working up some comic business: Parolles made 'a joke entrance', walking to the top of a shallow flight of steps before he realised he had forgotten his sword, then making a foppish return. Guthrie had travelling bags thrown up on to the stage from the pit, and when on 'Little Helen, farewell' it came time for him to go, he gathered them up, together with a suitcase and a camera, returning each time Helena spoke to him during the twelve-line stichomythic exchange which follows. On 'That's for advantage', he finally slapped her on the bottom, whereupon she retaliated lightly with a little pat on his cheek: 'So is running away.' Nunn shifted to comedy when Stephen Moore made an entrance as a 'dandy decorated in white scarves like a walking Christmas tree' (Michael Billington); he carried on stage all his clutter for travelling, while offstage was heard the sound of a car horn. Television's Angela Down received Parolles's assault with an inscrutable expression, which may have been wit enough.

Parolles's disquisition on virginity runs to inordinate length, and Helena's answers grow shorter and shorter. He speaks more like a pimp than a chorus, but if their conversation begins as frivolous badinage, his words increasingly seem to express her unspoken thoughts:

> It is not politic in the commonwealth of nature to preserve virginity. Loss of virginity is rational increase; and there was never virgin got till virginity was first lost. That you were made of is metal to make virgins. Virginity by being once lost may be ten times found; by being ever kept, it is ever lost.

Parolles moves in a little threateningly, and she begins to listen to him intently. The barrack-room bawdy is related to herself as well as to Bertram and his friends. And when she asks the pointed question, 'How might one do, sir, to lose it to her own liking?', she seems to be hinting at her most secret thoughts and foreshadowing her own actions. When Parolles said, 'Virginity, like an old courtier, wears her cap out of fashion, richly suited but unsuitable', Guthrie's Helena broke away downstage as if she had been stung; and after Parolles's 'Will you anything with it?', in the *New Arden* text G. K. Hunter punctuated the Folio's ambiguous 'Not my virginity yet' as 'Not my virginity; yet . . .', so that the actress might suggest that she was suppressing what was too intimate to be spoken aloud.

In the end, however, she bursts out in rapture, singing herself from prose into verse as her voice rises with her feelings. Her virginity is far from being a withered pear, and she turns all of Parolles's jibes to love:

> There shall your master have a thousand loves,
> A mother, and a mistress, and a friend,
> A phoenix, captain, and an enemy,
> A guide, a goddess, and a sovereign,
> A counsellor, a traitress, and a dear . . .

She runs through the catalogue of lovers' poetical endearments, and breaks into an ecstatic sequence of oxymora: 'His humble ambition, proud humility, / His jarring concord, and his discord dulcet . . .' On the broken sentence, 'Now shall he——', she sees that Parolles is looking strangely at her, and so drops back into the prosaic nonchalance of 'I know not what he shall.' These fragmentary lines give trouble to textual editors, but they act very well on the stage, since her rather lame ending is full of obscure suggestions that she would like to save Bertram from temptation at court, betraying another, even a maternal, interest in him.

The brutal exchange with Parolles is sandwiched between two soliloquies from Helena, and when Parolles has gone, she turns again downstage, returning to her former musing. But it is a new and resolute Helena that we see. Alone again, her imagination leaps ahead:

> Our remedies oft in ourselves do lie,
> Which we ascribe to heaven. The fated sky
> Gives us free scope; only doth backward pull
> Our slow designs when we ourselves are dull.

If her first soliloquy was romantic, this is realistic, hard-headed. The discussion of virginity, painful though it was, has left her with a serious determination. Like Cressida's first soliloquy after the witty dialogue with Pandarus, Helena's parting speech is a sonnet, the formal couplets lifting the sentiments beyond individual characterisation to a level of impersonality from which she seems to speak for all women. Those who are far apart in wealth and social station can perhaps come together, and the rhyming emphasises her new vitality: 'Who ever strove / To show her merit that did miss her love?' And when she exits she is resolved: the King's disease will be her way.

I.2: The King is dying

There follows the first court scene in Paris. As the Elizabethan stage can manage so well, the scene changes instantly from the private world of lonely Helena at Rousillon to a crowded stage and the public world of the King of France. The change is effected by a flourish of cornets, followed immediately by the regalia of a royal retinue ('divers Attendants') and the youthful 'lords', thus superimposing the public image upon the private. The King signals for letters to be brought to him—the first of the many that seem to flow between the three locations of the play, Rousillon, Paris and Florence. Payne had several lords discovered reading as if the post had just arrived, for the news is that Florence is at war with Siena and has called for aid from France. The King will refuse it, but permits his officers to serve abroad on either side. His words, 'freely have they leave / To stand on either part', produced an audible 'Ah!' of pleasure from the officers in Bridges-Adams's court scene. In Nunn's production the scene was set in a gymnasium of sorts, where a number of athletic young men were to be seen training, fencing, vaulting, all splendid young dandies from some Ruritanian court showing off in front of their ailing king in a wheelchair.

Accompanied by Parolles and Lafeu, Bertram also makes his appearance in Paris—'What's he comes here?'—and he looks dashing if in uniform. Yet even as he salutes and kneels to the King, his fine young figure reminds the King of the dead Count, and so of the past: he and the old Count had been soldiers together, and he particularly remembers the esteem in which his friend has been held:

> Who were below him
> He us'd as creatures of another place;
> And bow'd his eminent top to their low ranks,
> Making them proud of his humility
> In their poor praise he humbled.

[42]

This adds to the audience's expectations of courtesy in Bertram: 'Such a man / Might be a copy to these younger times.'

However, the scene is designed chiefly to introduce the ailing King. Barton had him carried in on a litter; Guthrie had him pushed on in a wheelchair; television discovered him in bed surrounded by counsellors reading despatches to him from abroad. We are to be witness to his low state of mind as he thinks of the old Count—'Would I were with him!'—and as he recalls what the Count said before he died, the play again touches the relationship of age and youth:

> 'Let me not live' quoth he
> 'After my flame lacks oil, to be the snuff
> Of younger spirits'.

Above all the scene demonstrates the state of the King's health. Payne justified his sudden remembrance of Gerard de Narbon— 'How long is't, Count, / Since the physician at your father's died?'—by first giving the King a spasm, and Willman had him almost collapse on, 'If he were living, I would try him yet.' He calls for help to leave, and several move to assist him. The sick king goes; more saluting, more cornets. The picture is one of age at its extremity, failing fast in the midst of such splendid youth and vitality.

I.3.1-118: Back to Rousillon

The subject is again to be Helena, and a conversation is caught in progress, as the opening line by the Countess to her Steward ('Rinaldo') suggests: 'I will now hear; what say you of this gentlewoman?' Our perspective on Helena is to be extended, first through the cynical eyes of Lavache, and then in a report from the Steward that he has evidently been waiting impatiently to give. All this is to prepare the audience for a scene of most moving intimacy between the older and the younger woman. However, comedy is the bridge, the longwindedness of the rather pompous Steward, careful of his reputation, set in contrast with his opposite, the quick-witted clown and his scatalogical casuistry.

At the start Bridges-Adams had Lavache, cast as a gardener, draw attention to himself by singing, since he must sing again later in the scene; Willman had him play with a hoop. But a more authentic idea came from Payne: taking the hint from the line, 'If I may have your ladyship's good will to go to the world [i.e., get married], Isbel the woman and I will do as we may', he introduced business between Lavache and a giggling Isbel half hidden behind a curtain. On 'What does the knave here?', the clown produced her blushing and bobbing a curtsy. Subsequently he sang his jingle about Helen of Troy to this same Isbel: ' "Was this fair face the cause" quoth she / "Why the Grecians sacked Troy?" ' Though I have never seen it, the introduction of an 'Isbel' must help Lavache's antics in this scene, the pair of them lightly burlesquing Bertram and Helena.

It may seem from the Countess's words, 'Wilt thou ever be a foul-mouth'd and calumnious knave?', 'Get you gone, sir', and so on, that she is angry with Lavache, and the *New Cambridge Shakespeare* has her stamp her foot at him. However, one of his tasks is to moderate the Countess's sterner role of setting standards of behaviour and preserving the social conventions, by having us see her generously allowing the weaknesses of others. In criticising the reticence of Andrew Leigh in the part at the Old Vic in 1921, John Francis Hope in *The New Age* argued that Lavache makes the Countess laugh herself out of judgment, 'and he does not do it by lecturing like Dryasdust on the social problem. Lubricity should lubricate the wheels of being, and reduce friction' (15 December, p. 82). The text demands that he be shocking, and his 'foul-mouth'd and calumnious' talk about mating is surely designed for us to keep half a critical eye on Helena, just as his cynical little song about Helen of Troy is sung at the expense of Helena of Rousillon. Like Mercutio's bawdy before the balcony scene in *Romeo and Juliet*, it disarms our distrust of any sentimentality to come.

The Steward is a self-opinionated household spy bursting to tell a secret, and after Lavache has gone, he moves closer to the Countess for his confidence, 'I know, madam, you love your gentlewoman entirely.' So he speaks of overhearing Helena confess her love for Bertram, and he does so at length and with relish. Barton placed this scene *after* Helena's confession, but it is altogether a richer experience if the audience knows that the Countess knows the truth about Helena before she tells it.

I.3.119-47: Helena confesses

Perhaps the most sensitive scene in the play is this encounter between the old Countess and her young ward, in which the Countess elicits from her a confession of her love for her son. It is lightly done, with the gentle humour of the older woman guiding our view of Helena's predicament without destroying our sympathy for her. In performance, the variations to be played upon so realistic a situation are many, as they would be for an equally delicate and oblique scene in Chekhov. Helena is shy, embarrassed, fearful of losing the love of the Countess and destroying her chances with her son. The Countess is maternal, kindly and sympathetic, but also a little autocratic and quick of temper where she senses deceit. The scene reveals more of Shakespeare's insight into the female mind.

The playwright arranges a long entrance for Helena on to the Elizabethan platform, the time it takes the Countess to speak nine rhyming lines in soliloquy. The first Cambridge editors explained how this allowed Helena to enter 'with slow step and downcast eyes' as the Countess watched her; in *The New Cambridge Shakespeare*, however, Quiller-Couch missed the stagecraft preserved in the Folio and argued that Helena must enter at line 127 if there was not to be an awkward pause. Experience with the thrust stage has proved the earlier version right. It is important that the audience hears the Countess speak of her own experience in youth at the same time that it watches Helena enact the mood in pantomime, almost a Brechtian effect which is lost inside the proscenium arch if Helena makes a lateral entrance. It was lost on television when the camera merely cut to Helena on the Countess's cue, 'I observe her now.' Willman achieved the effect at Stratford-upon-Avon by having Helena walk on a garden terrace in silhouette across an illuminated skycloth. The lines begin,

> Even so it was with me when I was young.
> If ever we are nature's, these are ours; this thorn
> Doth to our rose of youth rightly belong;
> Our blood to us, this to our blood is born.

The rhymes lend the strength of common wisdom to the Countess's reminiscing, and are totally lucid: Quiller-Couch thought that an audience could hardly be expected to know that 'these' referred to the pangs of love, but an audience has no difficulty following a slight gesture towards Helena, and a glance upstage at the diffident girl as the Countess speaks has the effect of applying the sentiments to both of them. In Canada, Margaret Tyzack also fingered a red rose taken from the garden in which she sat, so matching the verbal suggestion of 'our rose of youth', the colour also picking up the sense of 'our blood' (i.e., our desires) and 'love's strong passion'. An even more powerful effect is secured if Helena herself carries the rose as the Countess speaks, thus binding the two experiences of unrequited love verbally and visually.

Helena arrives at the Countess's side and kneels or curtsies, and in her modesty begins a long evasion of the questions put to her. The girl's difficulties begin from the moment when the Countess anticipates her thoughts by saying, 'You know, Helen, / I am a mother to you', and the lines that follow call explicitly for a strong reaction:

> When I said 'a mother',
> Methought you saw a serpent. What's in 'mother'
> That you start at it?

In *The New Arden Shakespeare* (p. 28) G. K. Hunter explains that the words 'mother' and 'daughter' also imply 'mother-in-law' and 'daughter-in-law' for the Elizabethans, and to acknowledge the double meanings Willman and Barton had Helena turn her head away quickly in order to hide her feelings. Guthrie had her enter running, only to stop dead on, 'I am a mother to you', the first mention of the word. Helena's reaction is immediately tearful— 'this distempered messenger of wet'—and with pauses and hesitations she tries to find reasons for her behaviour without giving away her feelings about Bertram: 'The Count Rousillon cannot be my brother: / I am from humble, he from honoured name.' In his *Shakespeare III, 1599-1604*, Gareth Lloyd Evans thinks that Helena displays 'a volatility of temperament' in this scene, 'cautious, almost mulishly taciturn' in her first replies, but at the end her 'veering moods and attitudes are ... very much the result of her awareness of her social inferiority' (p. 64).

The evasions continue pathetically, although, sharing all their secrets as we do, not without making us smile. On 'You are my mother, madam; would you were—', Helena may kneel partly to dispel doubts about her loyalty to the Countess, partly to plead her case. But when the Countess speaks the unambiguous line, 'You might be my daughter-in-law', Helena must look away or even move away in her embarrassment ('What! pale again?'). The Countess may be more comforting—moving towards her, touching her arm or cheek on 'I am a mother to you', 'Yet I express to you a mother's care' and 'I say I am your mother', the repetition inviting a vocal caress; she may lift Helena's tearful face on, 'What's the matter ...?', and Catherine Lacey in Barton's production gave Helena a handkerchief with which to wipe her eyes. The confession may be precipitated, as in Guthrie's productions, which had Helena slide to the floor weeping when the Countess said, 'Yet I express to you a mother's care'; or it may be delayed, as in Barton's production, by having Helena resist any breakdown right up until she hears the provocative 'daughter-in-law'.

The crisis comes when the Countess puts the issue directly: 'You love my son.' Helena may move away quickly, and, as the lines suggest, her 'cheeks' and her 'eyes' will betray her—she will lower her eyes and try to cover her face with her hands. In the long speech of the Countess beginning, 'Yes, Helen, you might be my daughter-in-law', there are many hints at Helena's possible reactions, but finally the Countess presses home her advantage with a series of sharp questions:

> — Speak, is't so?
> — Do you love my son?
> — Love you my son?
> — Go not about.
> — Come, come, disclose / The state of your affection.

In this interrogation, Guthrie had Edith Evans hold Zoe Caldwell's hands to give her confidence; Willman had Rosalind Atkinson fire the questions at Joyce Redman from downstage, so that the audience could see her face. Richard Eder of *The New York Times* described how in David Jones's production Martha Henry received the questioning from Margaret Tyzack: 'She equivocates, twists this way and that, and finally falls to her knees with an audible crash and the marvellous directness of her line, "Before you, and next unto high heaven, / I love your son" ' (9 June 1977). Whatever subtleties are adopted, the basic pattern must have the Countess authoritatively at ease, in contrast with an agitated and stumbling Helena. The long cross-questioning serves to make the girl totally human and vulnerable.

When the truth is out, the Countess will fall back, relaxing her pressure with an 'Ah!' Now Helena's words gush out without restraint as she throws herself on the mercy of her guardian. The stage is Helena's, and she may move away half in a dream ('I know I love in vain, strive against hope'), and then return to the Countess half in supplication ('My dearest madam, / Let not your hate encounter with my love'). At the last, Shakespeare smoothly returns to the earlier motif, and has Helena appeal to the older woman's memories of her own youth:

> but if yourself,
> Whose aged honour cites a virtuous youth,
> Did ever in so true a flame of liking
> Wish chastely and love dearly that your Dian
> Was both herself and Love; O, then, give pity
> To her whose state is such that cannot choose
> But lend and give where she is sure to lose.

This touches the Countess on a sensitive spot, and she in her turn is the one to react with momentary embarrassment. This is the turning point. She relents, lifts Helena to her feet and asks whether she has already made a plan to go to Paris.

The last part of the scene is thus in part given to furthering the plot, and with new resolve Helena may sit on 'I will tell truth' (Barton's Helena returned the handkerchief), disclosing her intention to cure the King, and so in fact to be near to Bertram. But there is more. With 'Why, Helen, thou shalt have my leave and love', the Countess gives her such a blessing and embrace as to suggest that she is actually reliving her own story. At this moment the feelings of the two women are in tune, and Muriel St Clare Byrne had only praise for the way Edith Evans and Zoe Caldwell played the scene in 1959: 'In their concerted playing we saw the youth of the Countess live again as she claims the girl as the child of her spirit. The cycle of experience completes itself under our eyes' (p. 560).

ILLUSTRATIONS

I

II

III

IV

V

VI

VII
VIII

ACT II

II.1.1-91: The King is worse

The play returns to Paris; for the Elizabethan stage, 'flourish cornets' again. After the supposed passage of time suggested by the change of location, doubtless the King seems a little closer to death. This was hardly true of Benthall's comedy of fainting fits and hypochondria, as described by J. C. Trewin in *The Observer*: the King was 'nightgowned, on a litter, his crown over a nightcap' and 'surrounded by a pack of physicians who would seem to be ancestors of Molière's Dr Diafoirus' (20 December 1953). The simple and realistic way of indicating that the King's health has deteriorated is to have his hand fall lifelessly from time to time, like William Hutt's at Stratford, Ontario in 1977. On television, Donald Sinden lay in bed being bled, and Bertram himself held the King's limp fingers to be kissed by his subjects.

Shakespeare makes nothing of dividing the lords into those who will fight for Florence and those for Siena (the 'Sennoys'), and this matter holds no importance for the Tuscan service or the rest of the play. But as the young gallants begin to take their leave in high spirits among themselves, kissing the King's hand before saluting on exit, Shakespeare supplies several cues for the performance of the dying man. He bids God-speed to an abundantly healthy set of young blades who are itching to get to the war, and the incongruity is acute when they refer to his health. His little joke about 'those girls of Italy' (ironically foreshadowing Bertram's amorous adventures in Florence, although of course it is Helena, the French girl, who tricks him) must seem pathetic on his lips. The loud chorus of laughter from his boisterous audience comes nicely just before he feels more pain and calls for help: 'Come hither to me.' The *New Cambridge Shakespeare* believes that the King faints on this line, and Willman had Alan Webb play it so, but there is nothing in the lines to suggest that the lords react to such a faint. Some editors have him helped off the stage at this point, but again there is no call for this, since the large platform of the Globe could accommodate more than one centre of action. The focus now simply shifts from the King and his attendants to Bertram as he stands apart with Parolles and his other friends.

Without quite turning it to farce, Guthrie questionably

lightened the tone of the scene's opening by introducing comic business for Parolles. The braggart was anxious to pay his respects to the King by springing to attention when the sick man was passing in his wheelchair, and so fell off the steps to the stage. Later, Guthrie had the King give Parolles a 'double take' when he saw him again, and Parolles nodded and waved like an old acquaintance, only to be nearly run down by the wheelchair. When footmen served glasses of wine to the departing men for a toast to 'His Majesty', Parolles was unlucky enough to be passed over twice as the tray came round. The danger in such comic business is that it can reduce our sense that the King's end is near, and grief and foreboding will cast less of a shadow over the valedictions. Helena must be able to convince us that she is about to face a true test of her courage and special powers.

In the smaller group, Bertram is shown to be much more at home with his contemporaries, but he is still not one of the rest. He is 'commanded here', and it is even possible that he should remain in civilian clothes for his court scenes. Nevertheless, the audience is to be given an advance warning of a reason for his subsequent desertion of Helena. He is soon persuaded to leave with the others and, prompted by the ebullient Parolles, he makes up his mind: 'By heaven, I'll steal away.' The congratulations that follow come to a sudden stop with the approach of the King, now recovered from his fit: 'Stay; the King!'

Lafeu, who we remember has accompanied Bertram to Paris, enters to bring news of Helena's proposal. He is evidently amused by the idea that a young girl can effect a cure, and the King's illness becomes the subject of light joking. Their somewhat wry humour merely emphasises the fact that Lafeu is bringing the King one last hope of cure, a hope so slim that the two must jest about it. The repartee even becomes smutty as Lafeu tempts his master with the thought of Helena:

> I have seen a medicine
> That's able to breathe life into a stone,
> Quicken a rock, and make you dance canary
> With sprightly fire and motion.

The King chuckles, and this undercurrent of bawdy at Helena's expense persists as she shyly enters the royal bedchamber and Lafeu, pantomiming Pandarus the go-between, pulls her in: 'Nay, come your ways' . . . 'I am Cressid's uncle, / That dare leave two together.' So the two old men provide a perverse and incongruous overture to the scene of curing the King, isolating Helena again and challenging the audience's expectations.

II.1.92-209: Curing the King

Too realistic an approach to this unprecedented scene must sap the poetry and diminish the imaginative range of the lines. Barton's first Helena, Estelle Kohler, was for example a tease of a girl behaving in a very modern way; according to Hilary Spurling in *The Spectator*, she was 'perched on the bed and rumpling up the blankets to titillate the dying King' (9 June 1967). It was in this scene that the spatial neutrality of Guthrie's thrust stage came into its own, but even when transferred to the proscenium stage at Stratford-upon-Avon, the healing of the King, according to *The Times*, soared with the rhyming couplets and seemed to possess a touch of the supernatural: 'The like of a fairy-tale magic plays over the scene between the King and the young woman who stakes her life on his cure. Trick it may be, but we accept it as something more' (22 April 1959).

The Helena of the Elizabethan stage makes a long timid entrance: the King's ironic 'This haste hath wings indeed' tells us how slowly she must approach him; Payne had her turn and retreat in fear as soon as she entered. Lafeu's repeated 'Nay, come your ways' are words spoken both to a novice in a brothel and to a recalcitrant child. However, when Lafeu has gone the jocularity ceases abruptly and a solemn atmosphere descends. The old King and the young girl are alone in each other's presence. Helena is silent and the King is again close to death, so that the audience should begin to feel the tension, and the magic, between them. In his introduction to the *New Arden* edition, G. K. Hunter draws attention to 'the traditional association of virginity with magic power and priesthood' (p. xlii), and so Helena's ambiguous role as a whore and a priestess permits the sexual banter to suffer an extraordinary transition as she begins to practise her incantations. To induce the religious atmosphere, Willman had the candles on his stage carried off and lowered the lights.

Helena's curtsy, low and slow as befits the pace of the scene, helps at once to dispel the ribaldry and to show her respect and humility. The King may gesture her to sit on a stool at his feet, as with Guthrie. Her voice dips as she speaks first of her father, but she recovers to announce her mission clearly. The King again conveys his pain and despair, and Guthrie's Robert Hardy spoke with broken speech, stopping and starting as he sat at a table writing, suggesting that his mind had by now no firm grip on the situation; he turned and looked up at Helena on 'labouring art can never ransom nature / From her inaidable estate' as if surprised that she was still there; and he pointed his magnifying glass at her threateningly when he seems to accuse her of being an 'empiric' (a quack). Helena makes as if to go: 'I will no more enforce mine office on you.'

This is the moment that Shakespeare chooses to shift his play into couplets again. An aura of the magical descends upon the action, a quality which G. Wilson Knight in *The Sovereign Flower* explained as 'the gnomic, formal, incantatory quality of the rhymes, functioning ... as the language of inspiration' (p. 152). The verse and the voices together acquire a new sonority, and to assist the religious effect it would not be out of place to introduce harmonious music gently into the scene, as Shakespeare does in *King Lear* when Cordelia wakes the King from his madness, and in *The Winter's Tale* when Paulina commands the statue of Hermione to step from its pedestal. The King seems to relent and speak more kindly:

> I cannot give thee less, to be call'd grateful.
> Thou thought'st to help me; and such thanks I give
> As one near death to those that wish him live.

To indicate his acquiescence, Robert Hardy offered Helena his hand to kiss, as did Willman's Alan Webb: it was the cue for Helena to go to work. In the performance of this scene the audience is to perceive the two levels of the action, the realistic and the romantic, the psychological and the fantastic; in practice it is a balance hard to achieve.

For the realists, Barton had Helena begin her ministrations like an efficient nurse tending her patient. On Helena's line, 'So holy writ in babes hath judgment shown, / When judges have been babes', Estelle Kohler *closed in* on Sebastian Shaw's couch, transferring the idea of 'baby' to the old man and seeming to mother him. He resisted her attentions, however: 'I must not

hear thee. Fare thee well, kind maid; / Thy pains, not us'd, must
by thyself be paid', and threw a cushion in irritation. With her
even more rhythmical lines beginning,

> The greatest Grace lending grace,
> Ere twice the horses of the sun shall bring
> Their fiery torcher their diurnal ring . . . ,

Kohler placed a soothing hand on the King's forehead and
encouraged him to lean back on his pillow. Television's Angela
Down delicately touched his brow with the tips of her fingers.
This kind of therapy then began to work immediately. On
Helena's 'What is infirm from your sound parts shall fly, / Health
shall live free, and sickness freely die', Shaw sat up, and when he
said, 'Methinks in thee some blessed spirit doth speak / His
powerful sound within an organ weak', he was on his feet. Upon
the line, 'Sweet practiser, thy physic I will try', Helena produced
a phial from her waist, although it seemed hardly needed, and
on, 'Give me some help here, ho!', he quaffed the potion and left.
On television, Donald Sinden dwelt lasciviously on Helena's
'youth, beauty, wisdom, courage', and as she touched him, he
caressed her face and neck before pointing his line 'Unquestion'd
welcome and undoubted blest' with an erotic kiss.

Nunn's second Paris scene took place in elegant clubland, and
Helena (Harriet Walter) first confronted an irritable King of
France (John Franklyn-Robbins) over a card-table in a busy,
realistic setting of 'green shaded lamps, brandy glasses and soda
syphons on the gaming tables'. She was soon kneeling before him
as he sat testily in his wheelchair, her head first in profile and
then turning towards the audience for her moment of ritual. At
this point Stanley Wells felt that Walter's performance, though
graceful and often touching, missed some of its poetic power:
'She is not helped by having to deliver the incantatory couplets
with which she works upon the King across a table full of brandy
glasses' (*The Times Literary Supplement*, 27 November 1981). She
finally wheeled him off briskly through a little crowd of
astonished attendants, dispelling any possibility of poetic ritual.

The remedy applied by Guthrie's Helena (and to a degree, by
Willman's) was rather less physical and more hypnotic. In both
the Guthrie productions the speech and movement were more
ritualistic and the gestures more mystical, and this treatment of
the lines picked up the quality of wistful fantasy that had been

struck in Helena's intimate soliloquies of the first act. Alec Guiness as the King was placed in his wheelchair centre stage rather unnaturally, and when Irene Worth as Helena began to speak her rhymes, 'What I can do can do no hurt to try, / Since you set up your rest 'gainst remedy', she made no attempt to approach the King, but *moved back* from him, kneeling down a little upstage of him like a priestess about to perform a sacred rite. At one point, the King seemed to falter in his faith: 'I must not hear thee. Fare thee well, kind maid', and Worth accordingly retreated like an angel banished, turning only at the exit to talk of 'the help of heaven'; Willman's Joyce Redman knelt down as if to utter a little prayer. All this compelled a response from the King, and when Helena said, 'But know I think, and think I know most sure, / My aim is not past power nor you past cure', he relented and, as it were, gave his consent for the ceremony to begin.

The cue for Helena's intoning lies in the phrase 'inspired merit', meaning 'divine inspiration', almost 'the breath of God', so that the intervention of Providence is implied in her actions. Worth began an incantation with the lines, 'Ere twice the horses of the sun shall bring / Their fiery torcher his diurnal ring', the style sufficiently archaic to suppress any sense of realism. Redman picked up the beat of the metre and moved rhythmically on the repetition, 'Ere twice in murk and occidental damp / Moist Hesperus hath quench'd his sleepy lamp'. Worth walked slowly behind the King and placed healing hands on his forehead, until he closed his eyes and sighed: no need of a potion to drink—the touch of her fingers was enough. The steady rhythm of the lines may even suggest that Helena circles round the King, casting a spell in some primitive witchcraft. But hers is no invisible, offstage miracle: the magic is all done in full sight of the audience, who will see the means and the end for themselves.

Let Muriel St Clare Byrne in *Shakespeare Quarterly* for autumn, 1959 describe how Zoe Caldwell cured Robert Hardy in Guthrie's production:

> Miss Caldwell makes a quick and unexpected move, stands behind the King's chair, and places her hands on his brow. He makes an impatient gesture as if to brush aside her insolent presumption—their timing throughout this passage was perfection—stops at her invocation of 'the greatest Grace', relaxes, closes his eyes and listens, while with a subtle, barely perceptible rise in tone into

what is practically recitative, she speaks the couplets, with their fanciful, stilted phrasing, as an incantation, a charm; and carried beyond herself, rises to the crucial answer upon which her life and fortune depend, and wrings from the so-called fustian rhymes a moment of pure theatre magic and spell-binding. It is quite breathtaking, and completely right, startling and convincing us simultaneously. (p. 563)

The King finally speaks his most reassuring lines, 'Methinks in thee some blessed spirit doth speak', sighing and touching Helena's restorative hand. Guiness slowly brought Irene Worth round to face him, until she knelt and kissed his hand: 'If I break time, or flinch in property / Of what I spoke, unpitied let me die.' There is now new strength in the King's voice, and Helena herself sounds a new note of resolution, her former character transformed:

> *King.* Make thy demand.
> *Helena.* But will you make it even?
> *King.* Ay, by my sceptre and my hopes of heaven.
> *Helena.* Then shalt thou give me with thy kingly hand
> What husband in thy power I will command.

Some enchanting agency has effected the cure. It is not yet complete, however—'Give me some help here, ho!' is the exit line of one who is still unable to walk alone. The real *coup de théâtre* is planned for the next entrance of Helena and the King.

II.2: The Countess and the Clown

Omitted completely by Benson, Benthall, Guthrie and Willman, and much trimmed by everyone else, this short scene in prose has been considered expendable because of its obscurity and its bawdy, and because it does little for the plot. It has been called 'silly stuff' (John Dover Wilson) and 'almost pointless' (Glynne Wickham). It was written, I feel sure, to allow time for the principals to change costume and prepare for their coranto, while neatly requiring the audience to wait in anticipation. It is also written in a style chosen to relieve the heavy atmosphere with its wit and provide a spirited transition to the major scene of comedy in which Helena picks a husband; in so far as the scene to come is overshadowed with disaster, the Countess's scene is a nicely misleading device. She and Lavache are the only ones who will not be in Paris to see the cure completed, and so it is they who provide the bridge; otherwise the plotting is quite perfunctory—she orders her servant to the court with a letter for Helena.

That said, Lavache's talk of buttocks, French crowns, taffety punks, cuckolds, scolding queans, nuns and friars certainly strains the dignity of the Countess, who must play 'straight man' to the comedian. For no apparent reason other than to extend the picture of home life in Rousillon, Moshinsky had Lavache eat soup during the interview: Elizabethan clowns are strangely tolerated by their employers, but this may be going too far. Nor is there this time an Isbel provided as a target for Lavache's wit, and his lines are all directed at the Countess. Some—'He that cannot make a leg, put off's cap, kiss his hand, and say nothing, has neither leg, hands, lip, nor cap'—call for him to pantomime as he speaks, and suggest a strongly physical performance. Performance also explains the Folio punctuation of the Countess's 'An end sir to your business: give Helen this', which is preferable to the modern editor's 'An end, sir! To your business: give Helen this'. This line, incidentally, prompted Bridges-Adams to have the Countess offer to beat Lavache with her stick, until she finally chased him off on his mission with, 'Haste you again.'

Payne introduced business for the lady herself. When she said, 'I will be a fool in question, hoping to be the wiser by your answer. I pray you, sir, are you a courtier?' she dropped a mock curtsy to Lavache, and so started a series of antics to go with his repeated catch-phrase, 'O Lord, sir!' According to William Warburton, the eighteenth-century editor of Shakespeare, this is 'a foolish expletive then in vogue at court', and no one since has been able to improve on this explanation. In *Early English Stages*, Glynne Wickham believes that it helps the audience to take the measure of Parolles by having the clown parody the way the braggart will handle a court conversation in the next scene (vol. III, p. 198); however, Parolles does not in fact say these words. The phrase was evidently used to answer any question, which implies that it must be spoken each time with a different inflexion in order to raise a sequence of laughs. The actor playing Lavache who can do this successfully today will be rare; a natural clown will presumably have less trouble, and in 1981 Geoffrey Hutchings was genuinely funny.

II.3.1-181: Choosing a husband

This outstanding scene, sometimes called 'the suitors' scene' and sometimes 'the recantation scene', constitutes the climax of what might be thought of as 'the first movement' of *All's Well*.

Shakespeare has prepared the action carefully: the audience anticipates a miracle, and now the stage must effect it in its own terms. His *coup de théâtre* is to exhibit the change in the King's circumstances physically and spiritually—from a limp into a coranto, from a sickroom to a ballroom, from death to life. Of all the productions considered in this study, Guthrie's on the Ontario stage most struck this contrast by turning his open space into a dance floor, presenting almost the whole company in the elegant formality of an Edwardian court in evening dress and mess dress, and choosing a whirling Viennese waltz played by a full orchestra. The visual and aural surprise also exploited Shakespeare's couplets and captured the balletic spirit of the verse, so that Brooks Atkinson of *The New York Times* felt that the performance flowed 'without effort across the apron stage up and down the stairs, through the forest of columns and out of the posts in the pit' (16 July 1953). In this production the scene came naturally to be known as 'the ballroom scene', and Guthrie's treatment of the same scene on the stage of the Memorial Theatre at Stratford-upon-Avon retained something of the same animated effect.

The stage represents the throne-room of the King of France, although television began the scene in an antechamber. It will be set with at least a throne, and the court made up of lords, officers and attendants enters in groups until the stage is full—all this before the King enters himself. Bertram is present with the rest, although he is conspicuously almost a silent figure. His silence, while not complete (he has three words, 'And so 'tis'), has been enough to worry editors and managers: Bell's edition of 1773 omitted him, as did John Philip Kemble in 1793 and 1815 and Henry Irving in 1888 in their editions. The Globe text, like C. J. Sisson's, rearranged the speeches to reduce Parolles to an echo, but in *The Arden Shakespeare* G. K. Hunter makes the sound observation that Parolles's continual intrusions encourage the comedy in Lafeu's attempts to speak to Bertram (p. 50, note). However, Bertram's silence may also suggest that he is standing apart, displeased with Helena's sudden rise to fame, and to indicate this Bridges-Adams had him move to one side. G. Wilson Knight's comment in *The Sovereign Flower* was simply that 'Any able producer would make full use of Bertram's silent, sulking presence' (p. 155).

Lafeu's first line is 'They say miracles are past', and in spite of Parolles's Osric-like foppery, it is Lafeu who sets the tone here and elsewhere in the scene. The King's cure is the 'very hand of heaven', he declares, and he carries a sheet of paper, a broadsheet or a ballad published in the customary Elizabethan way to mark the special occasion; it is entitled, 'A Showing of a Heavenly Effect in an Earthly Actor'. Bridges-Adams went one better and introduced the scene with the ringing of church bells. Guthrie decided that the moment had come to lift the whole play on to another plane, and gave the impression of inventing a new scene: on the Stratford, Ontario platform he had twenty supers enter from all points of the compass, making good use of the new vomitaries in that theatre, and on the Memorial Theatre stage they entered from promptside and opposite promptside, from upstage and from the pit, all discussing the King's recovery and uttering words like, 'The King is cured' and 'A miracle, a miracle'. In this way Guthrie took up Lafeu's suggestion that Providence had taken a hand, and the repetitions of the insatiable Parolles with his 'So I say . . . so I say . . . so say I too . . . so would I have said . . . I would have said the very same . . . so I say . . . I would have said it' effectively contributed to the high spirits of the court. All voices rose to a pitch of excitement before the entrance of the King.

It is important that the King and Helena should make a sensational entrance into the crowded court, and the fact that the scene is framed by a discussion between Lafeu and Parolles implies that Shakespeare is using them as a device to direct our response.

    Parolles. . . . Here comes the King.
    Lafeu.   Lustig, as the Dutchman says. I'll like a maid the
               better, whilst I have a tooth in my head. Why, he's
               able to lead her a coranto.
    Parolles. Mort de vinaigre! Is not this Helen?
    Lafeu.   Fore God, I think so.

These two comment on the vigour of the King and imply a new image for Helena, while Shakespeare supplies the cue for the coranto with its energetic high-stepping. The dance captures the mood of the scene, and marks the King's cure and his new relationship with Helena. It is strange that editors have been puzzled by Lafeu's 'Fore God, I think so', since we are surely to see Helena transformed along with the King. She is now a girl radiant with the prospect of securing her beloved Bertram, and no doubt her mourning costume will be replaced by brighter colours (Irene Worth and Zoe Caldwell wore a springtime lemon yellow in Tanya Moiseiwitsch's design). There will be music, applause, cries, laughter, more applause.

The cue for the coranto is for music as well as dancing, but some directors have chosen to reduce the intended effect. Bridges-Adams neglected the music and had a trumpet announce the King's entrance; Helena knelt to him before sitting to one side of his throne, glancing at Bertram as she did so. Moshinsky introduced the dancing without the music, with the King and Helena seen in long shot prancing down a corridor; Payne introduced music without the dancing, and both productions had Helena sit beside the King on a second throne. Willman had the King lead Helena impressively down a flight of steps for their entrance. Barton used trumpets again, and his courtiers danced a minuet. Only David Jones had William Hutt and Martha Henry effectively perform the coranto. Nunn opened the scene with a stage alive with waltzing couples, into which the King danced with Helena. Guthrie went for the full theatrical effect, using an on-stage orchestra which 'galloped into a waltz' when the King spun Helena on to the stage to the applause of the assembled court. Her brilliant crinoline was set against the King's black evening dress, and, surrounded by exquisitely turned-out gentlemen and officers, the splendidly ceremonious effect prepared the stage for the imminent crisis.

The King goes immediately to the work of granting Helena her choice:

> Go, call before me all the lords in court . . .
> This youthful parcel
> Of noble bachelors stand at my bestowing,
> O'er whom both sovereign power and father's voice
> I have to use. Thy frank election make;
> Thou hast power to choose, and they none to forsake.

His concluding couplet lends a nice formality to the occasion, and the 'lords in court' may well step briskly forward. How they line up will affect the manner of the choice, and help the audience anticipate its outcome. There must be a minimum of five, including Bertram, and to be aware that his turn is still to come, the audience must see him standing at the end of the line, where they can watch his reactions of increasing disbelief and horror as his chances of being chosen grow stronger.

The business of choosing a husband takes the form of an ironic competition in which the winner is known from the outset by Helena and the audience. The basic action may be outlined. On 'Thy frank election make,' Helena rises from where she is sitting and moves centre stage. There she curtsies to the company, as if making up her mind, and begins by addressing the assembled lords evasively. The King prompts her a second time: 'Peruse them well.' The Folio has here, 'She addresses her to a lord', suggesting that she turns to the first young man. But it is a false start, and as if she is still uncertain how to manage the situation, she again speaks to all of them, unable to come to the point: 'Gentlemen, / Heaven hath through me restor'd the King to health.' Moshinsky's lords here applauded politely. Again she falters:

> I am a simple maid, and therein wealthiest
> That I protest I simply am a maid.
> Please it your Majesty, I have done already.

And so she backs off and turns away.

The action to this point is realistic in manner, as if Helena's modesty and vulnerability are transparent in her simple words and repetitions. But Shakespeare chooses this moment to shift his play into rhyming couplets again, so stylising the speech and movement. The King prompts Helena a third time: 'Make choice and see: / Who shuns thy love shuns all his love in me.' Television had Helena's next lines, 'Now, Dian, from thy altar do I fly ...,' spoken 'voice over' as if she were summoning up her courage. The repeating pattern of movement to each lord is now quite artificial, a flirting motion of advancing with a curtsy to each man, who bows his acknowledgment. Helena rejects each one with another curtsy, and may even exchange a laugh with the fourth on 'You are too young, too happy, and too good ...' The lines invite a charming and stylish dance. Nevertheless, Helena never quite takes her eyes off Bertram. Nunn staged the scene like a child's elimination game of musical husbands, with the men circling round Helena to the music, which, when it stopped, cut them out one by one until only Bertram was left.

In order to emphasise the irony of the situation, Shakespeare again uses Lafeu to provide a commentary on the action, although the playwright's intentions have been differently interpreted. When each lord accepts Helena, she makes a polite refusal—she wants Bertram, of course. But Lafeu instantly jumps to an incorrect conclusion and indignantly assumes that it is they who have rejected her. He is deceived because she wants to hide her intentions and does not let the court hear what she says. Bertram is to be kept in the dark for as long as possible, and he and the audience will first see the action as the world sees it and as Helena would have it seen, that is, through the eyes of Lafeu. He begins by asserting Helena's merits:

> I'd give bay Curtal and his furniture
> My mouth no more were broken than these boys',
> And writ as little beard.

Then he reacts to what he takes to be shocking discourtesy on the past of the lords:

> —Do they all deny her? An they were sons of mine I'd have them whipt; or I would send them to th' Turk to make eunuchs of.
> —These boys are boys of ice; they'll none have her. Sure they are bastards to the English; the French ne'er got 'em.

Moshinsky had Lafeu whisper his asides into the ear of the King, thus incensing him before Bertram's refusal.

In his 1765 edition of Shakespeare, Dr Johnson commented, 'None of them have yet denied her, or deny her afterwards but Bertram. The scene must be so regulated that Lafeu and Parolles talk at a distance, where they may see what passes between Helena and the lords, but not hear it, so that they know not by whom the refusal is made.' In the Cambridge edition, Quiller-Couch thought this was right, although he believed that Johnson had not completely understood. He therefore added,

> There are four young lords besides Bertram drawn up in a line in front of the chairs upon which the King and Helena sit. She rises and, after a blushing speech to them all, addresses each in turn, passing along the line as she does so. The irony of the situation, as is clear from their replies, is that all three lords who do speak are very ready to accept this delightful maid at the King's hands. So evident indeed is their intention in their eyes, that Helena is

obliged to be abrupt with the first, and to put words of refusal as it were into the mouths of the other three. The fact that Lafeu, standing at a distance, misunderstands what is going on, has misled the commentators. That all the wards but Bertram should desire her is both good nature and good drama. (p. 146)

Another interpretation came from Joseph Price in *The Unfortunate Comedy*. He believes that the lords all accept Helena's advances, but speak with frigid formality in order to obey only the letter of the King's injunction, while 'the other courtiers bow graciously and relievedly away' (p. 156). In the *New Penguin Shakespeare* (p. 179) Barbara Everett agrees with him, and in her introduction to *The Riverside Shakespeare* text Anne Barton adds the comment that 'the constraint and inner fear at the prospect of being chosen by Helena' reflect the class-conscious snobbery of the wards of court, and it is this that is mocked by the more generous Lafeu (p. 500). In other words, the young men are all Bertrams under the skin. If this were true, it would underline the normality of Bertram and the boldness of Helena.

Nevertheless, it is unwise to fly against the direct evidence of Shakespeare's words, and Guthrie had no trouble in justifying Quiller-Couch's judgement in his edition, that 'despite her blushes, Helena thoroughly enjoys this interview of the candidates for her hand, and to overlook her gaiety is to miss half the charm of the episode' (p. 148). In *Shakespeare Quarterly* Muriel St Clare Byrne gives some idea of the lighter vein in which Guthrie produced the scene in 1959: 'Technically the difficulty of staging this gay little comedy passage, in which the supposed wooer herself phrases each apparent approach as a courteous rejection and gains courage from the young men's evident admiration and disappointment, is that it has to appear to Lafeu as if they reject her, and his angry asides have been taken literally by several editors.' And Byrne goes on to explain how the staging made it possible to believe that Lafeu had seen but not heard the exchanges between Helena and the young men. Each individual encounter was treated 'as a pas-de-deux in a cotillion which removes them from earshot to the further side of the stage for the brief encounter. The change in the manner of the dance when she comes to Bertram is most interesting—from a gay, waltzing turn to a more formal, angular, almost tango-ish step, which breaks the mood and prepares for the

harshness of his rejection of her. The total effect is brilliant'
(p. 566).

There is temporary confusion on stage, and we must assume
that it was intended by Shakespeare. Whether or not the lords
want Helena to choose them, whether or not Lafeu is right in
thinking that they are ungallant, whether or not Helena is
pleased or fearful that she will be prematurely accepted,
ambiguity is part of the excitement of the scene. To see with the
eyes of the audience, as the playwright himself must, is to be
struck by the accumulation of ambiguities to which the lords,
Lafeu and Helena all contribute, so that nothing seems quite
certain until the crisis. However, as so often in comedy, the
audience knows more than the characters and has the strongest
sense of the outcome, even if it cannot anticipate Bertram's
reaction. It enjoys the mistake Lafeu is making, and becomes a
willing participant in sustaining the suspense of the moment.
Thus one feels that Guthrie was right: to have reduced Helena's
momentum at any point before she reaches Bertram must check
the impulse of the play's first movement towards their expected
collision. To that end, in Guthrie's elaborate choreography, she
danced with no fewer than six men before coming face to face
with Bertram.

Helena's provocative behaviour with the lords is a form of
flirtation, but it is all pretence: she knows what she wants. The
critical moment comes when Lafeu announces, 'There's one
grape yet.' He indicates Bertram and seems convinced that the
Count neither can nor will refuse her. Yet, when it comes to it,
Bertram is taken by surprise, and, to judge by the peremptory
dialogue, even the audience is to take a degree of shock. Her eyes
dropping nervously, Helena curtsies to Bertram and hedges a
little as she does with the others. Her voice quavers as she says,
'I dare not say I take you . . .' Harriet Walter drew in her breath
sharply before she spoke. Then, for all to hear,

> *Helena.* This is the man.
> *King.* Why, then, young Bertram, take her; she's thy wife.
> *Bertram.* My wife, my liege!

Timing is of the essence here, but so powerful is the preparation
for this moment that it is difficult to go wrong. Bridges-Adams
had Lafeu shake Bertram to his senses, so stunned was he,
before he broke away, first taking a step towards the King and

then crossing past Helena in protest. On television, Ian
Charleson responded with a nervous laugh. Philip Franks flung
away, immediately losing his dignity. According to the
punctuation of the Folio text, which may be that of the actors
themselves, both Bertram's words and the King's are to come
out all in one breath:

> —Why then young Bertram take her shee's thy wife.
> —My wife my Leige?

Reality is to return with a rush, and the rhymes cease abruptly.

Guthrie chose this moment of truth to stop the music, just as
Helena and Bertram finish their dance on the forestage. On 'This
is the man', she led Bertram to the King, with people in the
crowd slapping Bertram on the shoulder and applauding as they
went. But he was not laughing, and his 'My wife, my leige!' was
spoken in anger. This stage-craft impressed all the reviewers,
and in *The Sunday Times* Harold Hobson described the effect at
Stratford-upon-Avon:

> Bertram is unperturbed [during the dancing]; he looks upon his
> companions serenely; he does not realize until the last moment
> that there is any danger of his being the favoured man. But when
> the choice falls upon him he shatters the formality by rushing to
> the steps of the throne, and unfolding the horror by which he has
> been overcome. The effect is very great; the artificiality that Mr
> Guthrie has deliberately induced is smashed by the reality of
> Bertram's assertion of individual independence; and a climax is
> created that Shakespeare could not but have approved. (26 April
> 1959)

The crowd gave voice: 'Shame! Shame!', and the presence of the
court accentuated, not the problem of 'a poor physician's
daughter', but the issue of loyalty: now Bertram and the King
face each other. Helena tried to stop the conflict at the outset,
running to the King on his line, 'Thou know'st she has rais'd me
from my sickly bed', only to be ignored. She dropped to the floor
beside the throne. The scene was now set for the public confrontation between monarch and subject.

For this is also the King's scene, and the challenge to his
authority, with his anger at Bertram's refusal, provokes the first
statement of values in the play. The King's speech on honour,
frequently trimmed in production, is a centrepiece, and for its

sake Shakespeare returns to couplets. The music and dancing have now stopped; the court stands silent. Beginning with restraint, the King from his throne speaks words that will be tested by what is to come. Robert Hardy lifted Zoe Caldwell to her feet on, 'From lowest place when virtuous things proceed, / The place is dignified by th' doer's deed.' Sebastian Shaw drew Estelle Kohler paternally to his side, where she sat. Robert Hardy then led Bertram by the arm downstage.

> She is young, wise, fair;
> In these to nature she's immediate heir;
> And these breed honour . . .
> If thou canst like this creature as a maid,
> I can create the rest. Virtue and she
> Is her own dower; honour and wealth from me.

At this, Guthrie's court came to attention.

In her essay, 'Virtue Is the True Nobility', M. C. Bradbrook has pointed out that the royal formula, 'Can you like of this maid?', implies, not love, but 'only the ability to live harmoniously together' (p. 298). However, even with such *ex cathedra* reasons Helena is aware that the King's wooing of Bertram on her behalf must diminish his esteem for her, and after an age of remaining silent, she tries again to intervene ('My lord!' was interpolated by Zoe Caldwell), kneeling to the King in an attitude of supplication.

Bertram. I cannot love her, nor will strive to do't.
King. Thou wrong'st thyself, if thou shouldst strive to choose.
Helena. That you are well restor'd, my lord, I'm glad.
     Let the rest go.

Guthrie's court stirred uneasily. Barton had his Bertram, Ian Richardson, pace up and down. But the King is now in a rage and will not yield:

> My honour's at the stake; which to defeat,
> I must produce my power. Here, take her hand,
> Proud scornful boy, unworthy this good gift,
> That dost in vile misprision shackle up
> My love and her desert; thou canst not dream
> We, poising us in her defective scale,
> Shall weigh thee to the beam.

Guthrie's King slapped Bertram's face on, 'Proud scornful boy', and his 'Here, take her hand' suggests that he has actually dragged Helena forward and thrust the two together.

Bertram finally 'recants', and he will kneel to the King on, 'I submit'. The actor's task is then to find a way to pronounce the key line, 'I take her hand', and indeed to take it, while all the time conveying his loathing to the audience. Shakespeare's accumulation of ironies will assist him. The King's reference to 'the staggers and the careless lapse / Of youth and ignorance' may produce a sign of assent from Lafeu. The murmur of the crowd may assume a tone of disbelief. Barton had Bertram kneel to Helena on

> I find that she which late
> Was in my nobler thoughts most base is now
> The praised of the King,

so that his gesture and voice could be construed as sarcastic. Guthrie had not Bertram but Helena hold out a hand, looking back at the King until Bertram took it. According to Roger Warren in *Shakespeare Survey 31*, David Jones had Nicholas Pennell offer Martha Henry 'a coldly formal arm, with a lip curled in distaste, as he led her offstage to the enforced wedding' (p. 145). Probably it is enough to utter the four dry words, echoing the King, 'I—take—her—hand', to make the contract totally ambiguous. To cap the bizarre moment, on the King's exit Barton had Parolles mockingly repeat Lafeu's first line, 'They say miracles are past', so undercutting the whole episode with irony.

At the last, all eyes are again on Helena. Moshinsky's Angela Down was close to tears. All through the King's harangue, she was an almost passive object: the impersonality of 'this creature', and of the King's instructions, 'take her', 'take her hand', 'take her by the hand', seem to make her more a chattel than ever. Bertram's response to the 'take—take—take' is of course to obey the literal order. Even when the King gives the peremptory command that the marriage ceremony be 'perform'd tonight' (at which Guthrie had an officer interpolate, 'Tonight, my lord?'), Helena speaks no further word. Nevertheless, as the audience watches these mechanical proceedings, her silence speaks for her.

II.3.182-293: Bertram the married man

The Folio includes an unexpected stage direction at this point: 'Parolles and Lafew stay behind, commenting of this wedding.' The recantation scene is to have a short coda, and it is not an uncommon device for Shakespeare to conclude a crowd scene by leaving two characters downstage to comment on what has passed. Bridges-Adams changed the set to 'another room in the palace', so tending to isolate Lafeu and Parolles and what they have to say. But their comic quarrel is here intended to lighten the atmosphere of the stage, to remind the audience of Parolles's continuing presence, and to prepare us to witness a sorry Bertram in his newly-wedded state. His decision to decamp unceremoniously for the wars follows immediately.

Lafeu touches a sore point when he first mentions Bertram's capitulation, and Parolles flies to the Count's defence:

Lafeu. Your lord and master did well to make his recantation.
Parolles. Recantation! My Lord! my master!
Lafeu. Ay; is it not a language I speak?
Parolles. A most harsh one, and not to be understood without bloody succeeding. My master!

Lafeu continues to tease, until Parolles loses his temper and they almost come to blows with 'Hadst thou not the privilege of antiquity upon thee——'. At this, Quiller-Couch suggested that Parolles lay his hand on the hilt of his sword in a theatening fashion; Moshinsky's Peter Jeffrey twice drew his sword on Michael Hordern, who brushed it aside with a laugh. When Lafeu appears to be making up the quarrel ('Give me thy hand'), Payne's Lafeu took Parolles's hand and twisted his arm, forcing him on to his knees; he then proceeded to pacify the braggart by force for several lines:

Parolles. My lord, you give me most egregious indignity.
Lafeu. Ay, with all my heart; and thou art worthy of it.

Lafeu has seen through his pretences as through a 'window of lattice'.

The older man departs in triumph, and Parolles's suppressed venom spills out when he is alone: 'Well thou hast a son shall take this disgrace off me: scurvy, old, filthy, scurvy lord!' He proceeds to threaten Lafeu behind his back: 'I'll beat him, an if I could but meet him again.' Such a boast is the time-honoured cue for the re-entrance of the enemy, and a horrified Parolles bumps into Lafeu as he comes back. This time Lafeu brings news: 'Sirrah, your lord and master's married.'

The next moment a distraught Bertram makes his appearance, and Quiller-Couch emphasises his distraction by marking his first two lines as asides:

> —Undone, and forfeited to cares for ever!
> —Although before the solemn priest I have sworn,
>   I will not bed her.

Guthrie had Bertram collapse crying into Parolles's arms for the climactic, 'O my Parolles, they have *married* me!' He is the victim of authority, of women, of all the world. Watching Guthrie's production at Stratford, Muriel St Clare Byrne remarked on 'the sheer, comic dismay and boyish frustration' of his speech, and added that 'his male freedom did not last long!' It was perfectly understandable that he should turn to male cameraderie with its 'horse-play and practical joking' as a way of escape from 'his own womenkind, with their standards, their claims, their unclubbable natures, and their lack of understanding of his simple, elementary idea of fun' (p. 564). And Parolles is quick with his advice that he and Bertram should run away:

> To th' wars, my boy, to th' wars!
> He wears his honour in a box unseen
> That hugs his kicky-wicky here at home,
> Spending his manly marrow in her arms,
> Which should sustain the bound and high curvet
> Of Mars's fiery steed. To other regions!
> France is a stable: we that dwell in't jades;
> Therefore, to th' war!

Barton had Clive Swift flourish his sword on 'Mars's fiery steed' and make four mock passes with it on 'France', 'stable', 'dwell' and 'jades'.

Bertram is eager to agree, as if he had been waiting for the order. He ignores the letters he has received from the Countess, and his last words tumble over one another in their short phrases, until he stops short to speak the black line in which he equates marriage with madness and his prospective home with the madhouse: 'War is no strife / To the dark house and the detested wife.' Thus at the end of this ugly little conspiracy our thoughts are left with Helena and 'her single sorrow', fixed in our minds by the rhyme. And as the two men hurry off, it is she who enters next, all unknowingly.

II.4: Helena hears the news

With sharp irony, Shakespeare gives us a brief glimpse of the newly married Helena dressed like a lady and a countess. He sets her in the mocking presence of Lavache the clown and Parolles the comedian. The latter takes his time before he breaks the news that Bertram is leaving her, for us an intolerable delay.

The scene begins with Helena's opening and reading a letter from the Countess, now 'my mother', delivered by Lavache. This letter is the first of several in the play that pass between the members of the family, letters which bring together, yet separate, Helena and the Countess, the Countess and Bertram, and Bertram and Helena. The bride is apparently in good spirits, laughing at Lavache's jokes, and the dialogue proceeds in a quick, light banter. The whole tone is inconsequential, while the audience awaits the bombshell.

The letter from the Countess was a dramatic decoy, for it is Parolles who brings the real news. He relishes his secret until, 'Madam, my lord will go away tonight: / A very serious business calls on him', and blank verse introduces a new tension into the scene. Although Parolles is dressed in all his regalia, there is no mention yet of the war—that will be another blow to come. For the present, he teases Helena with the unaccustomed colourfulness of his notion that this obstacle in the way of her wedded love will make fulfilment all the sweeter when it comes. His image is taken from, of all things, the distilling of perfume from flowers, whose process calls for 'restraint': 'Whose want, and whose delay, is strew'd with sweets, / Which they distil now in the curbed time.' The penny drops for Helena, but she hears all this without revealing her turbulent feelings, unrequited love mixed with her sense of guilt and apprehension. Her clipped and impassive answers are all obedience:

> —What's his will else?
> —What more commands he?
> —In everything I wait upon his will.

This stony Helena is the married woman, who must depart the court and return to an empty home.

II.5: The farewell scene

As for Parolles, he is beside himself with triumph, and Guthrie kept him onstage for this scene to gloat; he hid 'in the orchard' (as the promptbook put it) where he had the shock of half hearing Bertram and Lafeu talk about him before he emerged. Lafeu cannot believe that the Count sees fit to place trust in his companion:

> *Lafeu.* But I hope your lordship thinks not him a soldier.
> *Bertram.* Yes, my lord, and of very valiant approof.
> *Lafeu.* You have it from his *own* deliverance.

Lafeu is sarcastic, but he is fully prepared to make up his quarrel with Parolles, until the moment that he sees him. Lafeu's reference to 'his tailor' and 'his clothes' tell us that Parolles has indeed dressed himself in his finery. By the time Lafeu exits, he has made up his mind that he is a fop: 'Fare you well, my lord; and believe this of me: there can be no kernel in this light nut; the soul of this man is his clothes.'

This scene, like the last, also begins with a quick and casual prose dialogue, all in preparation for the bleak exchange to come. The audience is made doubly aware of Helena's hapless position, because, well before her entrance, asides from Bertram and Parolles remind us of the trick they intend to play on her:

> *Bertram.* Is she gone to the King?
> *Parolles.* She is.
> *Bertram.* Will she away tonight?
> *Parolles.* As you'll have her.
> *Bertram.* I have writ my letters, casketed my treasure,
> Given order for our horses; and tonight,
> When I should take possession of the bride,
> End ere I do begin.

In John Philip Kemble's time, the parting was characterised by a degree of decency, with Bertram taking leave of his wife warmly and reducing the sense of her inferiority. Nevertheless, Shakespeare intended the scene to be one of marked cruelty. In the twentieth century, the cruelty has by and large returned, and directors have made much of Bertram's view of marriage as a 'dark house' and of a wife as a 'clog'—the word used for the weight tied to the leg of an animal to prevent its running away. Parolles and Bertram are downstage when the latter uses this bitter term, 'Here comes my clog', and they and we watch Helena make her long entrance towards her husband full of her suppressed grief.

In a more realistic setting, Bridges-Adams had the two men sitting at a table when Helena entered, with Bertram slapping his boot with a cane to show how unfeeling he was; nor did he rise when his wife approached. Guthrie made more use of Parolles, and on Helena's entrance he made a gesture of silence to Bertram, so that Helena was compelled to speak her lines without ceremony, after a curtsy and an embarrassed pause:

> I have, sir, as I was commanded from you,
> Spoke with the King, and have procur'd his leave
> For present parting.

She displays complete deference towards her husband: we hear the repeated 'sir' ... 'sir' ... 'sir'—she is still the poor physician's daughter. And Bertram's lines are regular, formal and cold:

> You must not marvel, Helen, at my course,
> Which holds not colour with the time, nor does
> The ministration and required office
> On my particular.

He insists that she go home, giving her a letter for the Countess, and repeats the injunction three times. Willman showed more compassion: his Helena curtsied and was utterly submissive, but she seemed to fight off tears on, 'I am your most obedient servant', so that a slightly guilty Bertram awkwardly helped her up: 'Come, come, no more of that.'

Bertram is nevertheless brutally quick to turn away:

> *Bertram.* My haste is very great. Farewell; hie home.
> *Helena.* Pray, sir, your pardon.
> *Bertram.* Well, what would you say?

The woman will not go! and he must repeat, 'What would you have?' Helena persists pathetically until she must actually *beg* a kiss:

> Something; and scarce so much; nothing, indeed.
> I would not tell you what I would, my lord.
> Faith, yes:
> Strangers and foes do sunder and not kiss.

Her lines are choppy, and the Folio runs them together like prose. Angela Down faltered and spoke the word 'kiss' under her breath. It is a delicate moment on the stage, and, however it is treated, it is intensely moving, for although there is no suggestion in the text that Bertram and Helena do exchange a kiss, a perfunctory peck on the cheek would be as painful to Helena as no kiss at all. Payne actually allowed a kiss, but only under the mocking eye of Parolles, and Bertram quickly turned away. Bridges-Adams not only denied her the kiss, but had her sit and sob quietly as the curtain fell slowly to music.

Recent productions have made more use of Parolles, implying collusion between the two men. On 'Strangers and foes do sunder and not kiss', Willman had Bertram make a move as if he were about to kiss Helena, partly suggesting that he did not entirely lack compassion, when he heard Parolles make a small movement upstage. It was enough to make Bertram hesitate and retreat. Guthrie made his dependence on Parolles even more obvious by leaving Helena and Bertram alone on the stage for the parting moment. When he said, 'Farewell; hie home', Helena put her hand on his arm lovingly, and moved closer to him expectantly after 'What would you have?' The two were held in suspense as she said, 'Something; and scarce so much', but at that point Parolles re-entered carrying a travelling case and whistling. He set the case down and went out again, but his presence, however brief, was enough to kill Bertram's rising feeling, and he broke off with 'I pray you, stay not, but in haste to horse.' Roger Warren objected to this half-hearted treatment of a powerful scene, and in his paper 'Why Does It End Well?' argued that 'the kiss scene is so unflinchingly presented, that to play it with Bertram almost giving the kiss until recalled by a "psst" from Parolles, as happened in two recent productions, is a piece of cheap sentimentalism which only serves to remind us how searingly painful the original writing is' (p. 88). Any compromise with the deliberate heartlessness of the scene denies the strength of Bertram's portrait and the intensity required of Helena.

In Guthrie's production Parolles entered yet again, this time putting on his coat, at which point Bertram positively shouted his line, 'Go thou toward home, where I will never come', as if he were speaking more for Parolles's ears than Helena's. He ran off leaving the empty stage to a lonely girl who then walked slowly away in another direction. However, it is clear from the placing of Helena's exit in the Folio *before* Bertram's line that Shakespeare intended a different effect at this critical moment. In *The Unfortunate Comedy* Joseph Price believes that 'the warmly human and tenderly simple pleas of Helena for a parting kiss excites Bertram to embarrassed irritation ... Psychological realism, inner truth, and amusement are all served by Bertram's loud boast *after* Helena's exit:

> Go thou toward home, where I will never come
> Whilst I can shake my sword or hear the drum'. (p. 159)

Like a small boy, he speaks his mind best behind her back. So ends the cruellest scene in the play.

ACT III

III.1: The Duke of Florence welcomes the French

Thinking of sword and drum, Bertram has hastened to the war, and Shakespeare promptly anticipates what he will find when he reaches his destination. The brief appearance of a martial Duke of Florence and his troops in this scene is also enough to provide a backdrop for the women's scene to come. At Stratford-upon-Avon in 1981, the scene moved to the war zone with a flash and boom of guns, and a glimpse of Helena among a group of pretty nurses.

Early editors decided that this was an interior scene in the Duke's palace, but the location could effectively be in the field itself: 'much blood' has already been spilled. A military flourish, and the stage takes on a threatening aspect of armed Florentines led by a plated and helmeted commander speaking to 'two Frenchmen' (whom we see later as the two 'lords', both captains by the name of Dumain). The Frenchmen do not pretend to know much of the politics behind the fighting (and so, therefore, neither shall the audience), but as emissaries they characterise the Bertram and Parolles who have yet to arrive in Italy when they suggest that other young Frenchmen like themselves are 'surfeit of their ease' and will 'come here for physic'. The scene is fleeting (it was omitted completely by Kemble, Benson, Benthall, Houseman, Barton and Moshinsky), with the Duke speaking as he enters and as he leaves, and we return immediately to Rousillon.

III.2: Letters from Bertram

The return to Rousillon is a visual echo of I.3, which also found the Countess alone with her servants, and it is as melancholy in tone. The action is arranged to show the reactions of the mother and the daughter-in-law to the news of Bertram's defection, and Rousillon is again to be a place of mourning and regret. The scene concludes with a new and intensified view of the love-lorn Helena, and her decision to leave.

The Countess holds an unopened letter in her hand, for she fears the worst. She talks to herself, and goes straight to the point: 'It hath happen'd all as I would have had it, save that he comes not along with her.' Her sense of propriety and of order in the family prepares for her reading of the contents of the letter, and this itself is set in counterpoint with Lavache's quips— there is a faint irritation about her line, 'Let me see what he writes'—and the clown speaks bawdily of *his* change of heart over Isbel. His comic affectation of courtly manners and speech is a foil for the expressions of concern which pass over the Countess's face as she reads to herself.

When she reads the letter aloud, the audience hears what it knows, but it will nevertheless be surprised by its clipped and offensive tone: ' "I have sent you a daughter-in-law; she hath recovered the King and undone me. I have wedded her, not bedded her; and sworn to make the 'not' eternal . . ." ' The Countess is stunned. She is at first speechless, and sits or rises to match the new tone of anger in what she says: 'This is not well, rash and unbridled boy, / To fly the favours of so good a king . . .' Her thoughts are first on her son's disloyalty, second on the insult offered to Helena. Again Lavache is ready with an off-colour joke, this time about Bertram's questionable activities in love and war. But he also serves to draw attention to Helena's sorrowful entrance: 'O madam, yonder is heavy news within.'

With another letter in her hand, Helena appears accompanied by 'two Gentlemen', subsequently designated in the Folio as 'Fren. E.' and 'Fren. G.' *The New Cambridge Shakespeare* thought that they may have been intended as different characters from the two Frenchmen of the previous scene (p. 159); however, their talk of Florence would make it difficult to persuade an audience that they were. For Helena, it is another long entrance, and, if the Countess's assertion that her feelings will not 'woman' her is a cue for Helena's tears, it can be a moving moment when she sobs and throws herself at the Countess's feet in an agony of despair, as Zoe Caldwell did in Guthrie's production: 'Madam, my lord is gone, for ever gone.' Quiller-Couch suggested that when the Countess says, 'Think upon patience', she should take Helena in her arms, thus adding to the emotion they share. But there is another way. The presence of the gentlemen from Italy with their reminder of Bertram may well have the effect of suppressing Helena's feelings until she is alone. Payne, for example, ensured a more intense and restrained tone by having Helena emerge from behind one of his stage pillars and sit quietly at one side in answer to the Countess's 'Think upon patience.' In this way, with her terrible letter in her hand, Helena is a second focus of attention when the Countess asks for news of Bertram: 'Where is my son, I pray you?'

In Shakespeare's source for *All's Well*, Giletta sent messengers after Beltramo and then received his reply; Helena receives Bertram's cruel letter as soon as she arrives home from Paris. She now joins in answering the Countess's question by reading from this letter.

> Look on this letter, madam; here's my passport.
> [*Reads*] 'When thou canst get the ring upon my finger, which never shall come off, and show me a child begotton of thy body that I am father to, then call me husband; but in such a "then" I write a "never".'

'Here's my passport' hints that Helena is already thinking of leaving Rousillon like a beggar, and the Countess reacts with pity for her daughter-in-law and anger towards her son.

> I prithee, lady, have a better cheer;
> If thou engrossest all the griefs are thine,
> Thou robb'st me of a moiety. He was my son;

[75]

> But I do wash his name out of my blood,
> And thou art all my child.

With a decisive, 'He *was* my son', Bridges-Adams had her take her own letter and tear it up. She turns again to the messengers, but Helena continues to repeat her 'dreadful sentence' mechanically from the letter she holds: 'Till I have no wife, I have nothing in France.' The *Arden* edition correctly translates this to mean, 'Until Helena has ceased to exist Bertram can possess nothing in France' (p. 77), but it can also suggest that he has no intention of returning to France until his wife has left Rousillon.

All the while, the two Gentlemen, friends of Bertram, are listening. They provide an onstage audience witnessing for us his cruelty to his wife, and the public exhibition doubles the enormity of the act. They blush for him, and even more for Parolles, who stands condemned by the Countess's censure: 'My son corrupts a well-derived nature / With his inducement.' With the two men she leaves in grief and rage.

Helena is thus alone again for a major soliloquy, the centre-piece of her performance and her strongest appeal to our sympathies. On television Angela Down returned to her lonely virginal to lose herself in music. Zoe Caldwell slid weeping to the ground by the bench she had been sitting on, saying over to herself, ' "Till I have no wife, I have nothing in France." / Nothing in France until he has no wife!' But she seems to find strength in her next lines, 'Thou shalt have none, Rousillon, none in France; / Then hast thou all again', speaking of Bertram only with the respect due to his formal title. Then in an explosion of selflessness, she blames herself for the threat to his life:

> Poor lord! is't I
> That chase thee from thy country, and expose
> Those tender limbs of thine to the event
> Of the none-sparing war? And is it I
> That drive thee from the sportive court, where thou
> Wast shot at with fair eyes, to be the mark
> Of smoky muskets? O you leaden messengers
> That ride upon the violent speed of fire,
> Fly with false aim; move the still-piecing air
> That sings with piercing; do not touch my lord.
> Whoever shoots at him, I set him there;
> Whoever charges on his forward breast,
> I am the caitiff that do hold him to't;

And though I kill him not, I am the cause
His death was so effected.

For these lines, Maureen Shaw rose to her feet, Joyce Redman fell to her knees centre-stage. Helena makes no criticism of Bertram, nor does she see her departure from Rousillon as a sacrifice of herself. She thinks only of his safety. So she resolves to leave, but, unlike Giletta, makes no suggestion that she plans to follow him to Italy. She merely utters the same thought over again, 'I will be gone', 'I will be gone', 'I'll steal away', finally turning and winding her way offstage. 'Come, night; end, day. / For with the dark, poor thief, I'll steal away.' Darkness and intrigue is characteristic of all that is to come, and both Guthrie and Barton emphasised the centrality of this soliloquy by placing their one interval after Helena's slow exit, in effect making this speech the turning point of the production.

III.3: The Duke greets Bertram

The scenes continue to alternate between France and Italy, the domestic and the martial, the private and the public. III.3 affords the audience a glimpse of Bertram's arrival in Florence, although it was cut by Kemble, Benson, Benthall, Houseman and Moshinsky. Bertram is promoted by the Duke to be 'the General of our Horse', and the display of soldiery with 'drum and trumpets' is in contrast with the poignancy of Helena's soliloquy; for this reason, an interval falling between this scene and the last would deny the force of the juxtaposition. The scene also enacts a little of Helena's description of 'the none-sparing war', and seems to justify her fears that Bertram will be exposed to 'th' extreme edge of hazard'; however, where she deplored the dangers of the fighting, he now boasts about it.

This scene was Guthrie's opportunity to invent his elaborate piece of business (see p. 10 above). The Tuscan battlefield was transformed into the Western Desert of 1941 and the spirit of the dialogue turned to farce, in order to open the second half of his production in a wholly new and frivolous tone.

In the Folio stage direction, 'Enter the Duke of Florence, Rossillion, drum and trumpets, soldiers, Parrolles', we observe that Parolles brings up the rear, and the short scene ends with a speech from Bertram in Parolles's vein to 'great Mars'—he will prove 'A lover of thy drum, hater of love'. The exit line confirms his previous determination to abandon domestic bliss for the field of battle, but by its bluster it ironically anticipates the unromantic nature of his activities behind the lines.

III.4: Another letter—Helena's

This time the Countess has read the letter before the scene begins, and has her steward Rinaldo read it to her again; in this way the audience may listen to its contents and watch the Countess's reactions at the same time. On this occasion Lavache is not on stage: there is less and less cause for humour. From Helena's soliloquy we already know much of what her letter contains. She blames herself again for her 'ambitious love'; she wishes to bring Bertram back from the war; and she asks for his forgiveness. There is again no sign of revenge, nor of intrigue. However, the audience could not have guessed that she would have left Rousillon as a pilgrim to some far-distant shrine. Modern editors have taken the shrine of Saint Jaques to be that of Great Saint James at Compostella in north-west Spain, which would have been known to the Elizabethan audience; if it is, it is a long way from Bertram in Italy. We sense a mystery.

Helena's letter is a sonnet, and its rhymes grant it a lyrical quality we have not heard before. Her theme of dying for love, heard first at the beginning of the play (I.1.86), is sounded again, ' "He is too good and fair for death and me; / Whom I myself embrace to set him free" ', but the letter now carries with it a spiritual air, based as much on the purity of the sentiments as on the image of Helena as a pilgrim. For the moment, at least, she seems as remote and saintly as her sonnet, and the Countess speaks for the audience: 'Ah, what sharp stings are in her mildest words!'

The Countess regrets that Rinaldo did not stop Helena, that she had no chance to speak to her first. And her thoughts again turn hotly to Bertram. Can Helena's prayers now save him from the wrath of God? Rinaldo must write to him immediately to bring him home. The urgency of her 'Write, write, Rinaldo' echoes Helena's own 'Write, write' in the letter. Perhaps then she will also return, 'led hither by pure love'. This is the low point for the Countess, because the two people she loves most have parted, and she thinks she has lost them both:

> Which of them both
> Is dearest to me I have no skill in sense
> To make distinction.

She leaves the stage dejectedly, and we do not see her again before she believes Helena dead.

III.5: Helena the pilgrim

For a new spirit in the play, as well as a new pace in the action, two new characters are introduced, the 'old Widow of Florence' and 'her daughter'. These two will play key roles in Helena's attempt to satisfy Bertram's requirements if ever she is to be his wife in more than name. They are introduced in the company of other Florentines, 'Violenta, and Mariana, with other citizens', but since Violenta has no lines, and since in her last speech in the scene Helena refers only to 'this matron', 'this gentle maid' and 'this virgin', we must assume that Violenta's name was printed in mistake for Diana's.

The scene is essentially a women's scene, and we are to see the war through another set of eyes. The ladies are going to talk about the men, and a link with the foregoing soldiers' scenes is immediately supplied by the recognisable sound of 'a tucket afar off', the Duke of Florence's own fanfare of trumpets. The women have gathered to watch the passing parade of the Duke's troops, and the Widow calls her friends on stage: 'Nay, come; for if they do approach the city we shall lose all the sight.' In more realistic productions, the scene is a prime opportunity to fill out the social picture. Payne included an old peasant with a boy to sit at his feet; on his balcony he placed three 'serving girls' to ogle the soldiers who would pass below. His stage was alive with business: servants crossing at intervals, the old man and the boy eating a meal, a sentry coming to attention, two girls serving a tray of drinks. At Stratford-upon-Avon Guthrie turned the occasion to broad comedy, with Diana (Priscilla Morgan) and another girl (Diana Rigg) opening the scene with a quarrel. Television set the scene in a country kitchen, with the Widow and her daughter preparing food that called for much chopping and rolling. But the soldiers are not to be seen before the women have spoken, and another tucket conveniently explains their non-appearance: 'We have lost our labour; they are gone a contrary way.' From time to time the text calls for the sounds of the same military parade to be heard later in the scene.

In an excited little circle, the Widow and her friends gossip about Bertram's valiant deeds in the field. It is Mariana who raises the issue of his more amorous conquests, and of Parolles's work as a go-between. On television, a forlorn Mariana looked as though she had already been seduced:

> *Mariana.* ... Well, Diana, take heed of this French earl; the honour of a maid is her name, and no legacy is so rich as honesty.
> *Widow.* I have told my neighbour how you have been solicited by a gentleman his companion.

And it is Mariana who reintroduces the topic of virginity into the play, with the focus this time on the young Diana, aptly named after the goddess of chastity:

> I know that knave, hang him! one Parolles; a filthy officer he is in those suggestions for the young earl. Beware of them, Diana: their promises, enticements, oaths, tokens, and all these engines of lust, are not the things they go under; many a maid hath been seduced by them.

This is the very moment of Helena's entrance: 'Look, here comes a pilgrim.' Payne actually had Jean Shepeard enter early, on 'Many a maid hath been seduced by them', and sit at the bottom of some steps so that the audience could watch her closely when her husband's companion as being judged, and the question of virginity still under discussion.

The audience has been warned of Helena's pilgrimage, of course, but her appearance in Florence nevertheless comes as a surprise. In *Shakespeare's Comedies*, Bertrand Evans makes the point strongly. Helena's soliloquy in III.2 and the letter in III.4 paint the simple picture of a deserted wife leaving her home to visit some foreign shrine where she intends to die. In fact, like Giletta in Painter's story, she has apparently come to Florence to fulfil Bertram's conditions: 'The action of the play, in the very

middle of its course, appears diverted if not devoid of direction
... *Then, suddenly, we see Helena in Florence—the very city
which Bertram came to serve in the wars!'* (p. 149, Evans's italics).
It has been a common theme among commentators on the play
that the characterisation of Helena collapses from the time when
she appears in disguise as a pilgrim—so Mark Van Doren
thought in his *Shakespeare* of 1939 (p. 183); and T. M. Parrott in
his *Shakespearean Comedy* of 1949 found it 'hard to imagine the
Helena of the earlier acts stage-managing the complicated business of intrigue and deception that end the play' (p. 351). In his
essay 'Dramatic Emphasis in *All's Well That Ends Well*', Harold
S. Wilson is among the few who indicate that she chose to do
penance as a pilgrim, and comes innocently to Florence without
any suggestion of some other motive. The truth seems to be that
Shakespeare keeps Helena's thought and purpose in doubt; she
is to be no straightforward heroine of romantic comedy.

When Helena arrives in Florence as a pilgrim, the ambiguity of
her motives calls attention to itself. Has she chosen the shrine of
St Jaques le Grand, which after all the Widow hears named
without question, because it lies on the road to Bertram? At the
end of her first scene she had hinted at a hidden strength and
determination: 'Who ever strove / To show her merit that did
miss her love?' Were her 'intents' 'fix'd' after all? In that respect,
her character has at least remained consistent: she mourned the
departure of Bertram for Paris more than the death of her
father, and she followed Bertram there more to keep him in sight
than to cure the King. This more complicated Helena—less
passive, more brazen, far more her own mistress—emerges
again, and if she is less romantic, she is certainly more
enigmatic.

To appear as a pilgrim, Helena has a second change of
costume. After her momentary, and ironic, splendour as the new
Countess, she now reverts to plain clothes, even plainer than
those she wore as the old Countess's gentlewoman. She will also,
according to the sonnet-letter, travel barefoot, although I have
never seen this on the stage. Helena has never seemed so humble.
Maureen Shaw swayed a little from fatigue on her entrance, and
was helped to a seat on 'I thank you'. For Guthrie's more modern
scene, A. Alvarez reported in *The New Statesman* that she travelled 'panoplied in veils and surrounded by wicker baskets
through melancholy Edwardian stations' (15 April 1959). The

audience recognises her at once, of course, and, knowing more of her story than the women, it impatiently awaits her reason for being in Florence.

We are not to be told immediately. As soon as Helena has mentioned her pilgrimage, there is a diversion, and the Widow draws everyone's attention offstage to the 'march afar':

> Hark you! They come this way.
> If you will tarry, holy pilgrim,
> But till the troops come by,
> I will conduct you where you shall be lodg'd.

With her fussy excitement, Guthrie's Widow (Angela Baddeley) got a laugh on 'They come this way' as she ran to her balcony (and, incidentally, a bigger one on 'I think I know your hostess / As ample as myself'). And Shakespeare begins to compound the irony of Helena's disguise by making Bertram the subject of the conversation while she pretends not to know him.

> *Widow.* You came, I think, from France?
> *Helena.*   I did so.

Moshinsky's Widow (Rosemary Leach) paused suspiciously before she asked her question. It is a moment of tension. Jean Shepeard moved away uneasily downstage in order to hide her face at the mention of Bertram's name, and Helena actually tells a lie when she says, 'His face I know not.' So she wriggles out of the situation. In Guthrie's comic scene, she was helped by a giggling Diana Rigg who exclaimed in admiration of Bertram, while others responded to his bad reputation with a 'Tut, tut.' Nunn delayed the moment of tension and had his Widow (Gillian Webb) and the other Florentine ladies look hard at Helena when she said, 'I know his lady'.

The subject switches to Parolles and his coarse reports of Helena, and this prompts her to assert that Bertram's new wife has been faithful to him. It is a moment for the audience to recall her encounter with Parolles in the first act:

> all her deserving
> Is a reserved honesty, and that
> I have not heard examin'd.

We assent to the general verdict, as expressed by Diana:

> Alas, poor lady!
> 'Tis a hard bondage to become the wife
> Of a detesting lord.

Payne's Widow (Barbara Gott) seemed half to have guessed Helena's identity at this point, but Shakespeare here chooses to introduce another diversion. The Widow indicates her daughter: 'This young maid might do her / A shrewd turn, if she pleas'd.' Helena is at once alarmed with new fears, and Maureen Shaw rose to her feet at the thought of being betrayed.

Again the talk veers in another direction, but suddenly all the innuendoes come to a head as 'the whole Army' marches on stage, led by Bertram and Parolles in person. The original staging of this scene invites speculation, since it is one of troops passing in parade while the heroine must conceal her feelings; it is a scene reminiscent of *Troilus and Cressida*, I.2, in which Cressida and Pandarus watch the Trojan heroes returning from battle. In the Globe Theatre the women may have played on the balcony, leaving the platform free for the soldiers, but the distribution of the lines suggests that the women, especially Helena, would be better placed downstage, commenting on the men as they enter through one door and proceed on their way to the other. On the proscenium stage the women and the men will perforce be divided right and left; Bridges-Adams and Trevor Nunn had Diana stand on a stool to see better. Nunn presented his army in a parade with a brass band which marched awkwardly up and down the narrow proscenium stage. As it happens, the men need be seen only fleetingly, Parolles muttering about the loss of his drum, Bertram with his head in the air (Moshinsky indicated that time had passed by giving him a handsome military moustache and beard).

Helena flies into something of a fright. With affected ignorance, she asks, 'Which is the Frenchman?', and Diana's provocative answer—

> 'tis a most gallant fellow.
> I would he lov'd his wife; if he were honester
> He were much goodlier. Is't not a handsome gentleman?

—prompts a smothered and non-committal 'I like him well' from her. As twice before in the scene, Bertram is immediately associated with Parolles. To Diana the latter is 'that same knave', 'that same rascal', 'that jack-an-apes with scarfs'. When she refers to his doleful expression—'Why is he melancholy?'—Helena's thoughts are quickly on the dangers of war, and 'Perchance he's hurt i' th' battle' is a nice touch which reminds us of the girl we knew before. However, all her fears—of the war, of discovery—are undercut by Parolles at the last. In Guthrie's production he carried a bottle of whisky and pinched the girls so that they squealed and ran off, Diana among them. Mariana's 'Look he has spied us' is a cue for him to bow and perhaps to doff his cap (his 'courtesy'). Payne had the women drop ironic curtsies in return, and shout after him, 'Marry, hang you!' . . . 'And your courtesy, for a ring carrier!' Nunn here established a special relationship between Mariana and Parolles, who ostentatiously brought up the rear of the parade, and these two later continued a lovers' quarrel in pantomime in the Italian café setting: Mariana had run off, and Parolles later kissed her and made up, finally leaving her in tears trying to drown her sorrows.

So the men march off, and Helena is able to recover her composure. The thought that 'the amorous Count' has been soliciting Diana 'in the unlawful purpose' has been troubling her, and she seems to be conceiving a plan. At the last moment she turns to Diana: 'I will bestow some precepts of this virgin, / Worthy the note.' This is a 'pious sentiment' that 'seems proper for a holy pilgrim', in the view of Bertrand Evans in *Shakespeare's Comedies* (p. 156), but to a suspicious audience, and a somewhat thwarted one, there's more to it. We have not stopped looking for a reason why Helena is in Florence, and now the questionable activities of Bertram and Parolles themselves begin to suggest a device by which she can pursue her proper ends. When we see her again, her scheme is well under way.

III.6: The plot against Parolles

Willman named this the 'Dumain brothers' scene': at line 98 we learn that the two French lords seen before in Florence and Rousillon are brothers, and at IV.3.166 that their name is Dumain. These two change from being mere messengers, and grow in stature as they assume a certain choric function as commentators; as Bertram is separated from Parolles, they also increasingly usurp the avuncular role of Lafeu. For, at the very time of the reversal of Helena's fortunes, Bertram's re-education is to begin.

In camp or tavern the Frenchmen sit drinking with Bertram. It is a time for reflection. In Stratford, Ontario, Jones suggested a bitter winter campaign by having the officers huddle together in furs: the sunshine would return only when Bertram returned to Rousillon and learned his lesson. Television had the men drinking at a cellar table in flickering firelight, with Bertram quietly playing a mandolin. It was a candlelight conspiracy.

'Nay, good my lord . . .'—they have been talking confidentially for some time when the scene begins, and the subject is Parolles.

2 Lord.	Nay, good my lord, put him to't; let him have his way.
1 Lord.	If your lordship find him not a hilding, hold me no more in your respect.
2 Lord.	On my life, my lord, a bubble.
Bertram.	Do you think I am so far deceived in him?

The two Frenchmen had heard from the Countess that Bertram was being corrupted by his follower, and they now see fit to warn him of Parolles's reputation as 'a most notable coward, an infinite and endless liar, an hourly promise-breaker'. In suggesting that he might fail Bertram 'at some great and trusty business in a main danger', they anticipate the betrayal Bertram will suffer in the scene of Parolles's unmasking (IV.3). So the conspiracy conceives a 'particular action to try him', although Bertram's words are still spoken in the high spirits of practical joking. The plan is to have Parolles recover the regimental drum, something he had apparently already boasted he could do, and then to capture, blindfold and cross-question him. The cue for his entrance, 'Here he comes', was also one for Bridges-Adams's players to pretend indifference and strike up a song.

Parolles's entrance is an occasion for laughter: he has not been seen in this mood before. The *New Cambridge Shakespeare* adds the stage direction, 'affecting melancholy', and in his report in 'Plays Pleasant and Plays Unpleasant' for *Shakespeare Survey 8*, Richard David describes how in Benthall's production Michael Hordern adopted an extraordinary gait which brought down the house: 'a jobbling unco-ordinated motion, head bobbling forward between limp shoulders from which the arms dangled, feet flapping carelessly down in the abandonment of utter disgust' (p. 135). Since the drum went with the colours, its loss implied the loss of the regimental honour, and Parolles's affectation of mortification is a high point of comic caricature for the actor playing the part.

His delightful exhibition also provides the conspirators with their opportunity to press him further:

Bertram. How now, monsieur! This drum sticks sorely in your disposition.
1 Lord. A pox on't; let it go; 'tis but a drum.
Parolles. But a drum! Is't but a drum? A drum so lost! There was excellent command: to charge in with our horse upon our own wings, and to rend our own soldiers!

The extravagance of Parolles's outrage suggests that he is gesticulating, making patterns in the air with his arms to demonstrate the cavalry charge, the wheeling of the horses as they turn the wings, and the rending of the foot-soldiers. Angry at this criticism of his command as General of the Horse, Bertram apes his friend: 'Why, if you have a stomach, to't, monsieur. If you think your mystery in stratagem can bring this instrument of honour again into his native quarter, be magnanimous in the enterprise, and go on . . .' The phrases have the empty flourish of Parolles's own style of speech—'I will grace the attempt for a worthy exploit' . . . 'even to the utmost syllable of your worthiness'—and Payne's Lords picked up the tone and echoed Bertram's 'to't' and 'go on' until Parolles's blood was up. 'By the hand of a soldier, I will undertake it', he cries, and on the oath he shakes each man vigorously by the hand. Bertram's line, 'But you must not now slumber in it', tells us that this protracted comic business—together with, perhaps, the brandishing of a sword and a thrust or two on 'mortal preparation'—goes on at length, all in preparation for Parolles's delicious exit line, 'I love not many words.'

To give him his due, Bertram continues to doubt that his friend is the braggart he is said to be, but his companions are quick to point out the hollowness of his show of confidence. So they leave to prepare their 'sport' with the 'fox', and the scene ends with a reminder of the other stratagem Bertram has in hand—the seduction of Diana.

III.7: The plot against Bertram

Back to Helena, now alone with the Widow, and another short scene: the pace of the play continues to pick up. Shakespeare has eliminated unnecessary dialogue, for Helena has told the Widow of her identity before the scene begins, and already broached the subject of making use of Diana's services to thwart Bertram. Along with the Widow, the audience is given a quick idea of the plan, and Helena makes it clear that her purpose is to get the ring the Countess gave Bertram:

> This ring he holds
> In most rich choice; yet, in his idle fire,
> To buy his will, it would not seem too dear,
> Howe'er repented after.

Helena makes no mention of love and sex; she is efficiency itself.

She is also at pains to say that she is not risking the Widow's reputation 'in any staining act'—she must believe that 'the Count he is my husband'. However, to Bertrand Evans, and perhaps to the audience, the implication behind her scheme is morally ambiguous. Just as she went to Paris to cure the King and won a husband, 'now she will save the honour of two young people whose emotions are not as well controlled as her own—and by doing so will claim her husband for good and all. Says the Widow, "Now I see / The bottom of your purpose": it is also our own first view of Helena's purpose' (p. 156). The implication is that 'her pilgrimage was never meant for Jaques, but for Priapus'—to get the ring from Bertram's finger and a child of his fathering. She had arrived in Florence 'with head up, hard-eyed beneath her pilgrim's hood, alert for means to implement her ends' (p. 157).

If this duplicity is true, then at worst we see it through the Widow's eyes, quite light-heartedly. Angela Baddeley fanned herself thoughtfully, and was at first reluctant to give her consent, vigorously protesting her birth and reputation, and three times uttering a 'No!' as Helena spoke. Certainly, comedy is introduced when the Widow appears to be not averse to a little bribery. She says slyly, 'Y'are great in fortune', so that Helena responds with 'Take this purse of gold, / And let me buy your friendly help thus far.' A moment or so later she promises a dowry of three thousand crowns for Diana, and the Widow capitulates immediately: 'I have yielded.' In this way we are never to know for sure whether she actually concedes that the plan is 'lawful', although Helena insists that it is:

> It is no more
> But that your daughter, ere she seems as won,
> Desires this ring; appoints him an encounter;
> In fine, delivers me to fill the time,
> Herself most chastely absent.

Angela Baddeley gave vent to a long 'Oh!' Helena will preserve Diana's virginity, keep her husband from adultery, and secure her rights of consummation as a wife seeking to complete the legal marriage-contract.

Nevertheless, the questionable nature of the trick of substituting one woman for another in a man's bed, whether they are married or not, is echoed consciously in the riddling couplets with which Helena ends this scene of whispers and innuendoes:

> Let us assay our plot; which, if it speed,
> Is wicked meaning in a lawful deed,
> And lawful meaning in a lawful act;
> Where both not sin, and yet a sinful fact.

In the *New Penguin Shakespeare* Barbara Everett explains that the first two lines of the riddle deal with each of the partners singly, and the last line takes them together: 'Bertram intends adultery and accomplishes it in lawful cohabitation with his wife; Helena intends and accomplishes lawful cohabitation with her husband; both together succeed in making innocent an act that could have been in fact fornication or adultery' (p. 195).

As it happens, the audience is not to see the bed-trick, but it soon understands that tonight's the night. There is a cue for music when the Widow explains that 'Every night he comes / With music of all sorts, and songs compos'd / To her unworthiness'. The women look offstage in the same direction, listening to the sound of a lute. They perhaps embrace to seal their agreement. Then Helena's whispered, 'But let's about it', quickly takes them off and to their task.

ACT IV

IV.1: The ambush of Parolles

The first three acts of *All's Well* belong to Helena; with Act IV the focus shifts to Bertram. In his essay, 'Shakespeare's Mingled Yarn', Walter King argued that at this point in the play Helena's education is all but complete, whereas 'Bertram's, which parallels hers, has not yet begun' (p. 42). It begins with a vengeance by almost destroying Parolles, who must be suppressed before Bertram can stand alone. The result is a prose scene in which Parolles is ambushed by his fellow officers, a scene wildly funny in itself and one that provides a nice contrast with the urgency of Helena's scene before.

It is essentially an eavesdropping scene, of the kind that Shakespeare frequently introduces into his comedies. As such, a basic decision has to be made about the spatial relationship on stage between the gull and his eavesdroppers, so that when Parolles becomes the centre of attention the 'five or six other soldiers' may be seen and heard as well as Parolles himself. Shakespeare provides only one hint for the spectator's visual imagination, and it occurs in the first line: 'He can come no other way but by this hedge-corner.' The 'hedge-corner' is enough to transform the space around the projecting façade or the pillars of the Elizabethan stage into effective acting areas, but it may also suggest that a hiding-place on the big neutral area of its platform is not needed at all—the words themselves have supplied the location, and, in the fashion of the *commedia dell'arte*, the party of practical jokers may simply creep up behind their victim to listen to him and mock him behind his back, and never properly conceal themselves at all. The pattern is reminiscent of Malvolio's letter scene in *Twelfth Night* (II.5). In a more realistic production, Willman worked with a low wall: the conspirators crouched behind it and Parolles sat down in front. This wall lent itself to a good deal of comic business: at one point Parolles drank from a bottle of wine and then set it on the wall, whereupon a soldier hidden behind it helped himself to a drink; when Parolles groped for the bottle to take another drink, the soldier carefully put it into his hand. Guthrie had a truck on the stage, and the soldiers hid inside and behind it; when Parolles walked round the truck to see whether he was being watched, the whole gang was forced to push round in front of him. On television, Parolles lay down to rest on the floor of a barn, while the soldiers hid in its loft just above his head, so that the camera could catch everyone in the same shot.

When the scene begins, it is night; the lights are low; perhaps the sounds of an owl and crickets are heard; all is whispering and suppressed laughter. One soldier carries a drum, a comically noisy prop. Willman's men whistled each other to come on stage, gesticulating for silence. One of the French Lords takes the lead and the soldiers enthusiastically lay their plans. It is settled immediately that there is to be a great game with words, appropriately for a victim with the name Parolles.

—When you sally upon him, speak what terrible language you will; though you understand it not yourselves, no matter; for we must not seem to understand him . . .
—He must think us some band of strangers i' th' adversary's entertainment. Now he hath a smack of all neighbouring languages, therefore we must every one be a man of his own fancy; not to know what we speak one to another, so we seem to know, is to know straight our purpose: choughs' language, gabble enough, and good enough.

With much laughter, they all practise their gabbling together. As it happens, the Lord's advice that they should seem to understand what they say to one another without actually knowing what they mean, is also particularly helpful when it comes to speaking the nonsense language, for the game is to appear by gesture and tone to be making sense, the voice now angry and threatening, now quieter and more reasonable. I take it that the few words of gibberish that Shakespeare supplies are there merely to encourage the players to invent more of their own.

'Here he comes' is Parolles's cue to enter, and also the soldiers' cue to scatter to their places ready for eavesdropping. Parolles's entrance is a slow one: he is even more dejected than before, and his opening words, 'Ten o'clock', suggests that a bugle blows or a clock strikes before he speaks: 'Within these three hours 'twill be time enough to go home.' He thereupon sits himself down, clearly indicating that he has not the slightest intention of going off on some foolhardy enterprise to retrieve the regimental drum. 'I must give myself some hurts, and say I got them in exploit. Yet slight ones will not carry it. They will say "Came you off with so little?" And great ones I dare not give.' The lines are full of implied business, and no doubt with a huge grimace he pricks himself carefully with the tip of his sword.

So his 'soliloquy' proceeds lugubriously as he considers the alternatives to a self-inflicted wound. If he cannot talk his way out of the situation, he can slash his clothes, or break his sword, or—more desperate now—actually shave off his beard, or throw his fine clothes into the river, and swear he 'leap'd from the window of the citadel'. Willman had Keith Michell jump off a stool to test the general effect of this. Throughout the episode, Parolles's speech is deliciously punctuated by comments from the French Lord, even to a point where Parolles seems to be unwittingly answering a question he was not supposed to hear:

Parolles. Though I swore I leap'd from the window of the
        citadel—
2 Lord. How deep?
Parolles. Thirty fathom.

Finally Parolles has the idea of stealing one of the *enemy's* drums.

He is about to go off to do it when the soldiers realise that they must not let their bird out of the trap:

Parolles. I would I had any drum of the enemy's; I would swear I
        recover'd it.
2 Lord. You shall hear one anon.   [*Alarum within.*
Parolles. A drum now of the enemy's!

The joke comes when Parolles hears the sound of the very drum he was speaking of: the conspirators bang their drum (which I take to be the point of the Folio's 'alarum within'), and make him jump out of his skin. Barton had all his men rush upon Clive Swift shouting, 'Cargo, cargo, cargo!' 'Do not hide mine eyes', cries Parolles, another cue for business, and they seize and blindfold him. Guthrie had a sack thrown over his head.

The soldier playing the 'Interpreter' begins his fearsome patter in an atrociously thick foreign accent:

1 Soldier. Boskos thromuldo boskos.
Parolles. I know you are the Muskos' regiment,
        And I shall lose my life for want of language.

A neat point: it is galling for a man who has always used his gift of words to get him out of scrapes to find that no one can understand him, especially since he could save his skin by passing on information about the Florentine force.

> *1 Soldier.* Boskos vauvado. I understand thee, and can speak thy
> tongue. Kerelybonto, sir, betake thee to thy faith, for
> seventeen poniards are at thy bosom.
> *Parolles.* O!

For 'seventeen poniards', Guthrie's Interpreter, Peter Woodthorpe, merely pressed the point of a pencil to Cyril Luckham's chest. On 'O, pray, pray, pray!', Keith Michell dropped to his knees and raised his hands in an attitude of prayer, whereupon another soldier quickly tied them together. Payne's men broke into a debate, repeating 'Volivorco?'—'Volivorco!' until it was decided over the head of their trembling prisoner that he would be spared:

> *1 Soldier.*   Haply thou mayst inform
>   Something to save thy life.
> *Parolles.*   O, let me live,
>   And all the secrets of our camp I'll show.

And all the soldiers repeat 'Acordo linta' to signify their agreement as they lead off a now whimpering Parolles to the ominous beat of their drum (the Folio's 'A short alarum within').

The audience is thus given a few minutes' relief from this kind of farce, yet may anticipate more fun to come:

> Go, tell the Count Rousillon and my brother
> We have caught the woodcock, and will keep him muffled
> Till we do hear from them.

Payne's soldiers continued to gabble 'Acordo linta' and 'Volivorco' to one another as they made their exit, long after Parolles himself had gone. The language game could continue indefinitely, it seems.

IV.2: Seducing Diana

The scene between Bertram and Diana could have been touched with sentimentality and melodrama. Instead, its wit springs from the audience's pleasant knowledge that the apparently weak and helpless victim will deceive her handsome and well-born seducer. John Barton had Ian Richardson seem, in the words of Alan Brien in *The Sunday Telegraph*, 'rather endearingly clumsy and over-eager as he tries to seduce Diana (Helen Mirren) across an awkward and uncomfortable travelling trunk' (4 June 1967). The scene is essentially comedy.

Certainly Bertram shows himself to be an inexperienced Lothario. In Ontario, Guthrie had music playing, picking up what the Widow said at III.7.81-2, and Donald Harron entered in burlesque style with a bunch of flowers.

> *Bertram.* They told me that your name was Fontibell.
> *Diana.* No, my good lord, Diana.
> *Bertram.* Titled goddess . . .

His words are flippant at the start, and Edward de Souza tried to kiss Priscilla Morgan on his first line, but she adroitly dropped her head and the kiss landed on her forehead. If she laughs at him, this is his excuse to try to entice her in more honeyed tones, matching the air of parody in his lines:

> Titled goddess;
> And worth it, with addition! But, fair soul,
> In your fine frame hath love no quality?

On television, where the scene was shot without bodily movement from start to finish in back-lit profile, Ian Charleson began his assault on Pippa Guard by caressing her cheek. Priscilla Morgan was forced to push de Souza's hand away, until, on 'You are no maiden, but a monument', he finally made a lunge for her bodice. Bertram next tries Parolles's reasoning on the subject of virginity (I.1.129), only to get the worst of the argument:

> *Bertram.* . . . now you should be as your mother was
> When your sweet self was got.
> *Diana.* She then was honest.
> *Bertram.* So should you be.
> *Diana.* No.
> My mother did but duty; such, my lord,
> As you owe to your wife.
> *Bertram.* No more o' that!

She touches a sore spot, and Michael Denison pulled Jill Dixon towards him angrily on 'I love thee / By love's own sweet constraint', until she broke away from him with 'Ay, so you serve us / Till we serve you.'

Diana puts Bertram squarely in his place with her quick tongue, adding pathos by speaking of the roses and thorns, the passion and the pain, we heard before from the Countess (I.3.120-1):

> when you have our roses
> You barely leave our thorns to prick ourselves,
> And mock us with our bareness.

The Countess's roses of unrequited love have here changed to stand for the virginal vulnerability of the young girl who cannot resist her feelings. Writing in the Introduction to the BBC's edition of *All's Well*, Henry Fenwick thought that Pippa Guard brought a mischievous sexuality to her performance as Diana: 'Her virtue, one feels, is genuinely in danger—her feelings are too mixed for her chastity to be reliable' (p. 18). These roses will be recalled again by Helena herself when she takes her leave of Florence (IV.4.32).

Diana does not remain passive for long. Her task is also that of Bertram's re-education. She speaks more aggressively:

> 'Tis not the many oaths that makes the truth,
> But the plain single vow that is vow'd true.
> What is not holy, that we swear not by,
> But take the High'st to witness.

Her resistance to his blandishments may well arouse him, and Michael Denison took Jill Dixon's hands and pulled her to him as she retreated. Bertram's rising passion is clearly marked: 'Be not so holy-cruel ... give thyself unto my sick desires, / Who then recovers ... Say thou art mine'—echoing and foreshadowing Helena the physician, for it is not Diana but Helena who will cure him. Diana will seem to succumb to his entreaties, but she has chosen the right moment to make her demand of him: Helen Mirren let Ian Richardson embrace her, and then said unexpectedly, 'Give me that ring.' Now it is Bertram's turn to retreat:

> *Bertram.* It is an honour 'longing to our house,
> Bequeathed down from many ancestors;
> Which were the greatest obloquy i' th' world
> In me to lose.
>
> *Diana.*   Mine honour's such a ring:
> My chastity's the jewel of our house,
> Bequeathed down from many ancestors;
> Which were the greatest obloquy i' th' world
> In me to lose.

Touché!—the exchange is that of Diana's honour for Bertram's then.

So Bertram concedes. Ian Charleson dropped the ring into a metal cup with a clink. And Diana promptly gives him his instructions in a disarmingly businesslike manner: 'When midnight comes, knock at my chamber window . . .' The trap is to be sprung at precisely the same hour of night that Parolles was to have retrieved his drum (III.6.69). She also promises to return his ring, and meanwhile to give him another in bed, but her speech is cleverly ambiguous:

> And on your finger in the night I'll put
> Another ring, that what in time proceeds
> May token to the future our past deeds.
> Adieu till then; then fail not. You have won
> A wife of me, though there my hope be done.

Bertram is not to know that the ring she will put on his finger is in fact the one Helena received from the King. These rings, indeed, gather up magical properties with the rhyming couplets, and keeping track of them all is a tease for the audience, but part of the spirit of comedy in the play. Denison knelt and kissed Diana's hand to seal the agreement, well satisfied; de Souza comically undercut his embrace by looking at his watch; Gwilym left in triumph, humming to himself.

Thus the character of Diana springs to life before this scene is over; she changes from victim to victor, and we are here prepared for her larger function yet to come. In his essay, 'Dramatic Emphasis in *All's Well That Ends Well*', Harold S. Wilson believed that Diana 'is just sufficiently realized as a character to give us the sense that she is aiding and protecting Helena against the wickedness of Bertram, rather than that she is serving as her puppet to entrap him' (p. 231). In this scene, in which Helena is necessarily absent, Diana speaks for a side of Helena we should not otherwise know. Bertram departs contented, but Diana remains to speak a soliloquy of disgust at 'all men', and 'Frenchmen' in particular. She places Bertram exactly— 'Frenchmen are so braid' (such deceivers)—and is granted an unclouded view of her lover that could not be afforded to Helena herself. 'Only, in this disguise, I think't no sin / To cozen him that would unjustly win.' This concluding couplet was cut by Benson, Bridges-Adams, Benthall and Barton. Bridges-Adams had a slow, reflective curtain; in lighter vein, Guthrie's Widow Angela

Baddeley brought Priscilla Morgan a comforting glass of milk at the end of the interview.

The bed-trick, the substitution of Helena for Diana in Bertram's bed, must be presumed to take place offstage soon after Diana has made her exit. John Bouchard's production at Rice University in 1981 effectively pantomimed a symbolic substitution on a balcony above the stage, all done in shadowy half-light, and so brought the conspiracy against Bertram to a vivid climax. Left to the imagination, the bed-trick is nevertheless a mysterious, even mystic, act of darkness in which Bertram's lust is to become Helena's fulfilment.

IV.3.1-110: The brothers Dumain

The long and lively scene of Parolles's interrogation and Bertram's recognition of his friend's treachery is preceded by a strangely static choric interlude in prose, much cut in production. Linking the stories of Helena and Bertram, the two French Lords speak impersonally and almost out of character—and altogether too formally to be brothers. The interlude exactly covers the time of Helena's bed-trick and Parolles's ambush: the witching hour of midnight is twice more evoked. The Lords' speech provides a kind of philosophic commentary on what has been happening, and in the absence of the Countess, Lafeu and the King, they are now the ones who pronounce the values to which the audience can subscribe. They contribute to what A. P. Rossiter in *Angel with Horns* calls the play's 'moral reflectiveness': 'All the minor characters are minor moralists. The play is peppered with abstract ethical comments . . . and their effect is cumulative' (pp. 96-7). To counter this effect, Bridges-Adams had the Lords playing cards in the mess, and Willman had them drinking wine. Moshinsky, on the other hand, emphasised the abstract quality of the dialogue by backing it with the faint sounds of a 'cello.

The Lords have another duty also, to convey a few expository details which move the play along: (1) that Bertram has received an angry letter from the Countess, (2) that the seduction is thought to be in progress, (3) that the war is over, (4) that Helena is reported dead and (5) that Bertram has taken his leave of the Duke. Bertram enters excitedly to confirm all these points:

> I have tonight dispatch'd sixteen businesses, a month's length apiece; by an abstract of success: I have congied with the Duke, done my adieu with his nearest: buried a wife, mourn'd for her; writ to my lady mother I am returning; entertain'd my convoy; and between these main parcels of dispatch effected many nicer deeds.

It is then reported that Parolles 'hath confess'd himself' and 'sat i' th' stocks all night', a hint of what is to come.

So much for the plot. The Lords' comments, especially those on Bertram before he enters, are more interesting. They draw attention to the effect on him of reading the Countess's letter: 'he chang'd almost into another man'. The Count's spotty character then receives an analysis that is all the more biting for being spoken by his friends:

> *2 Lord.* He has much worthy blame laid upon him for shaking off so good a wife and so sweet a lady.
> *1 Lord.* Especially he hath incurred the everlasting displeasure of the King, who had even tun'd his bounty to sing happiness to him.

Nor, more surprisingly, do they approve his seduction of Diana: 'He fleshes his will in spoil of her honour,' and what they say is unexpectedly sanctimonious:

> *2 Lord.* Now, God delay our rebellion! As we are ourselves, what things are we!
> *1 Lord.* Merely our own traitors.

They want Bertram to see Parolles 'anatomiz'd', in order that the Count may 'take a measure of his own judgments'. The unmasking of Parolles is to be part of the lesson Bertram must learn: 'His presence must be the whip of the other.' And so they conclude,

> *1 Lord.* ... The great dignity that his valour hath here acquir'd for him shall at home be encount'red with a shame as ample.
> *2 Lord.* The web of our life is of a mingled yarn, good and ill together. Our virtues would be proud if our faults whipt them not; and our crimes would despair if they were not cherish'd by our virtues.

Perhaps no other comedy of Shakespeare so insists upon the

realistic balance of the virtues and the vices in its hero and heroine.

A point of great interest in this brief prelude is the news of Helena's supposed death, hinted in her own letters and 'confirm'd by the rector of the place'. The news is deliberately held back until other matters concerning Diana and the war are disposed of; it is then sprung upon us as the climax of the discussion: 'the tenderness of her nature became as a prey to her grief; in fine, made a groan of her last breath, and now she sings in heaven.' This announcement both surprises and does not surprise the audience, which after all enjoys some knowledge of Helena's deeper plan. Now and later we are to watch the effect of her death on Bertram himself. In *The Sovereign Flower*, G. Wilson Knight believes that it is this news of her death that is also part of Bertram's re-education: it 'may be considered to act on him as does that of Fulvia on Antony. The letter which, presumably, tells him of it affects him deeply: "There is something in't that stings his nature" ' (p. 129).

The tide begins to turn for Helena and her Bertram with the events of this night, and the pause in the action provided by this interlude grants the audience a moment's respite to assess their importance.

IV.3.111-317: The interrogation of Parolles

For all its sobering side-effects, 'this dialogue between the Fool and the Soldier', as Bertram calls it, has traditionally been the funniest scene in the play. In his *Dramatic Miscellanies* of 1783, Thomas Davies gives one of the earliest accounts of it, when the comedian Harry Woodward played Parolles in the mid-eighteenth century:

> The unbinding of Parolles, who looked about him with anxious surprise and terror, redoubled the bursts of laughter which echoed round the theatre. Woodward was excellent in the whole scene, but particularly in characterising Bertram and the Dumaines, whose feelings, upon the unexpected heap of slander which he threw upon them, served to heighten the scene. Bertram was most angry, because Parolles deviated very little from the truth in what he said of them; his lasciviousness, and his intrigue with Diana, he could not deny.

> In all our comic writers, I know not where to meet with such an odd compound of cowardice, folly, ignorance, pertness, and effrontery, with a certain semblance of courage, sense, knowledge, adroitness, and wit, as Parolles. He is, I think, inferior only to the great master of stage gaiety and mirth, Sir John Falstaff. (vol. 2, p. 40)

Taking the cue from the Second Lord, who had reported that Parolles 'sat i' th' stocks all night', Benthall had him continue there for the interrogation and the unmasking. Nunn had him in handcuffs. Bridges-Adams and Iden Payne put him on his knees between two soldiers, facing a table as for a court-martial. There exists another kind of cue in 'Hush, hush! Hoodman comes', the call of children playing blind-man's-buff, and the game with Parolles may prove to be a better one if in his blindfold he is able to move about and be pushed from man to man.

The baiting of Parolles begins with the language game we heard before. 'Portotartarossa' is heard in the sternest voice from the Second Lord, who assumes the role of officer in charge of the interrogation; for Moshinsky he thumped the table. The soldier acting as 'Interpreter' explains in a thick accent: 'He calls for tortures.' Nunn's interrogator scraped a fork on a tin plate to sound like the wheel of the rack. Threats continue—'Bosko chimurcho . . . Boblibindo chicurmurco'—and there is no limit to the meanings to be improvised with these sounds. Payne had the words repeated like question and answer, and Willman had a soldier mockingly kiss the Lord's hand on 'Boblibindo', only to get a kick for his pains.

The war is of course over, but Parolles does not know this, and eagerly reveals the number of the Duke's horse and foot, gabbling his answers in his frenzy of terror: 'Spurio, a hundred and fifty; Sebastian, so many; Corambus, so many; Jaques, so many; Guiltian, Cosmo, Lodowick, and Gratii . . .'—a wonderful jumble of names. Keith Michell tripped and fell to his knees in his excitement, and continued round the stage on all fours during his speech, ending between the Interpreter's legs. The Interpreter, meanwhile, solemnly pretends to write everything down. We note that the Lords and soldiers are having all the fun; Bertram is troubled, and does not speak to Parolles directly, only in angry asides to his companions.

Begins the naming game, in which Parolles's tormentors are, unknown to him, the object of his abuse:

1 Soldier.   Do you know this Captain Dumain?
Parolles.   I know him: 'a was a botcher's prentice in Paris, from
whence he was whipt for getting the shrieve's fool with
child—a dumb innocent that could not say him nay.

On this, the Second Lord has to be restrained by Bertram from
laying hands on Parolles. When they search his pockets, Bertram
actually encourages the reading of a letter they find there
without knowing its defamatory contents — it turns out to be a
poem from Parolles to Diana about Bertram himself, warning
her that her lover will not pay his debts. Parolles protests that it
was written for the sake of the girl: 'for I knew the young Count
to be a dangerous and lascivious boy, who is a whale to virginity,
and devours up all the fry he finds.'

If this scene is thought to echo the contest of wits between
Prince Hal and Falstaff after the Gadshill robbery in *Henry IV,
Part I* (II.4), Bertram wholly lacks Hal's wit and joy. He does not
find Parolles's treachery amusing at all: 'Damnable both-sides
rogue!' Bertram is quickly out of temper, and it is his turn to be
restrained. Payne's Raymond Raikes snatched the paper from
the Interpreter; Willman's Michael Denison swung at Keith
Michell's face and missed; Barton's Ian Richardson drew his
sword on Clive Swift, but one of the Lords managed to trip him
and relieve him of his weapon in time.

Bertram.   He shall be whipt through the army with this rhyme in's
forehead.
1 Lord.   This is your devoted friend, sir, the manifold linguist,
and the armipotent soldier.
Bertram.   I could endure anything before but a cat, and now he's a
cat to me.

The terror-stricken Parolles grows more and more anxious to
please the 'enemy', and when the subject returns to the character
of the Second Lord, Parolles spits out his venom with a will, his
imagination swelling as he speaks:

He will steal, sir, an egg out of a cloister; for rapes and ravish-
ments he parallels Nessus. He professes not keeping of oaths; in
breaking 'em he is stronger than Hercules. He will lie, sir, with
such volubility that you would think truth were a fool.
Drunkenness is his best virtue, for he will be swine-drunk; and in
his sleep he does little harm, save to his bedclothes about him; but
they know his conditions and lay him in straw . . .

Willman inserted his stage laughter in four places in this speech: on 'you would think truth were a fool', 'drunkenness is his best virtue', 'save to his bedclothes about him' and 'lay him in straw'. The invective is so delightful that even the object of its attack, the Second Lord, reacts in awe: 'I begin to love him for this.'

Finally, sentence of death is pronounced: 'Come headsman, off with his head,' and with much business they prepare to behead him. Both Bridges-Adams and Payne used a stool for a block and pushed his head on to it. Guthrie added drum-rolls. Willman delayed the crisis with much bowing, clicking of heels and growling. The Jonathan Miller production at Greenwich in 1975 played this moment of mock execution in the spirit of modern sadism. This is Parolles's final humiliation: he is in tears, on his knees, begging for mercy: 'O Lord, sir, let me live, or let me see my death!'—which raises a roar of laughter from those on stage, even though they are not supposed to understand Parolles's language. So the blindfold is removed at last. Released from the stocks, Benthall's Michael Hordern closed his eyes and fell straight backward, then slithered to the ground in a heap. Now every line should get a laugh:

> 1 Soldier. . . . So look about you; know you any here?
> Bertram. Good morrow, noble Captain.
> 1 Lord. God bless you, Captain Parolles.
> 2 Lord. God save you, noble Captain.

The stage is frozen—it is a comic tableau. To prolong the moment, Payne inserted more of the nonsense-language here: 'Throca movousus! Cargo! Cargo! Cargo!' Guthrie's Interpreter lit a cigarette.

Parolles is dumbfounded, huddled in his mortification. He does not speak a word until all but the First Soldier have gone, then at last, from the depths of his soul, comes his simple response: 'Who cannot be crush'd with a plot?' Seeing Robert Atkins's production at the Old Vic in 1921, 'H.G.' of *The Observer* considered that this line was the only unforgettable one in the play. In fact it caps the whole comic action of the scene, and would be laughable if it were only a meaningless grunt. As it is, it is also painful, for we share some of Parolles's bitterness, as we do that of Shylock, Malvolio and Lucio of *Measure for Measure* when they are crushed.

At the end, Parolles is left alone to nurse his wounded feelings.

Yet the final soliloquy turns the tables in its own way, and reflects his irrepressible spirit. It is in verse, and as it picks up energy, it changes to ringing couplets.

> Yet I am thankful. If my heart were great,
> 'Twould burst at this. Captain I'll be no more;
> But I will eat, and drink, and sleep as soft
> As captain shall. Simply the thing I am
> Shall make me live. Who knows himself a braggart,
> Let him fear this; for it will come to pass
> That every braggart shall be found an ass.
> Rust, sword; cool, blushes; and, Parolles, live
> Safest in shame. Being fool'd, by fool'ry thrive.
> There's place and means for every man alive.
> I'll after them.

'Simply the thing I am / Shall make me live' has the elasticity of Falstaff himself, and in his article, 'The Life of Shame: Parolles and *All's Well*', Robert Hapgood reported that in Charles Taylor's production at the Ashland, Oregon festival in 1961, Parolles vaulted to his feet on the line. And the exit line, 'I'll after them', is also a challenge. Payne's Roy Emerton chased after the others crying, 'Captain! Count! Captain!' Bridges-Adams gave Baliol Holloway a slow, thoughtful curtain. Guthrie's Cyril Luckham whispered the line to the audience confidentially. How he says it will contain the secret of his survival, be it as a fool or a fox.

IV.4: Helena leaves Italy

A brief return to Helena and her story. It is comforting to have a glimpse of her and to see that she is indeed alive. She, the Widow and Diana, all three, are preparing to travel—Willman and Moshinsky had them folding and packing clothes; Guthrie's Widow was in tears as she fetched Helena's birdcage and umbrella. The situation has been set up: 'I am supposed dead... My husband hies him home,' and Shakespeare reminds his audience of the hand of Providence still at work in Helena's affairs:

> Doubt not but heaven
> Hath brought me up to be your daughter's dower,

As it hath fated her to be my motive
And helper to a husband.

However, the scene ends mysteriously by looking forward to the end of the play. Diana is to endure some further experience under Helena's 'poor instructions', and the two girls may embrace to seal their agreement. But what are those instructions? The audience is not this time to know, but, like Diana, must have faith—'more of this hereafter'. The play's title and the proverb echo in the exit lines, reassuring us of a prosperous outcome: 'All's Well That Ends Well. Still the fine's the crown. / Whate'er the course, the end is the renown.'

IV.5: Waiting for Bertram

The scene once again belongs to Rousillon and the older generation, with Lafeu generously pleading Bertram's case to the Countess. We are being prepared for his rehabilitation, and Lafeu blames everything on Parolles: 'No, no, no, your son was misled with a snipt-taffeta fellow there, whose villainous saffron would have made all the unbak'd and doughy youth of a nation in his colour.' Yet as much as they regret Bertram's misdeeds, the two old people also mourn the loss of Helena, with the Countess particularly strong in her maternal feelings: 'If she had partaken of my flesh, and cost me the dearest groans of a mother, I could not have owed her a more rooted love.' We are being prepared for Helena's resurrection.

The clown Lavache is also present to lighten the gloom after his fashion. Bridges-Adams had him play a pipe, and Willman a guitar. In the banter between Lafeu and Lavache, Lafeu appears to play the 'straight man' to the Clown's quips, and in spite of having called him a 'shrewd knave, and an unhappy', gets on well with him. In *The Unfortunate Comedy*, Joseph Price offers a plausible reason for this. Lavache is another of the 'unsavoury' characters in the play 'who win acceptance despite their faults'. The Countess accepts him out of love for her dead husband—'My Lord that's gone made himself much sport out of him'—just as Helena accepts Parolles out of love for Bertram (p. 167).

Lavache contributes to our sense in the play of a realistic balance of good and bad.

In the spirit of general reconciliation, Shakespeare through Lafeu now springs a new surprise, and an ironic one: 'I was about to tell you, since I heard of the good lady's death, and that my lord your son was upon his return home, I moved the King my master to speak in the behalf of my daughter.' The King has actually given his blessing to another marriage for Bertram, as a way 'to stop up the displeasure he hath conceived against your son'. A fresh obstacle that Helena cannot have anticipated! Not only another bride, but one whom the Countess approves. The audience suddenly feels the pressure of time. Lafeu reports that Bertram will be home tomorrow, to which the Countess adds, 'I have letters that my son will be here tonight.' To top this, it seems she wants Lafeu's daughter to meet Bertram immediately. Payne sounded a post horn at this moment, and Lavache enters to announce that Bertram has actually arrived this minute.

The Clown's final jest is disconcerting. He mentions that Bertram is wearing 'a patch of velvet on's face; whether there be a scar under 't or no, the velvet knows'. This plaster covers either a battle scar or a surgical incision made to cure syphilis— Bertram is either a hero or a profligate. Lafeu believes he is the former, but Lavache's ugly word 'carbonado'd' implies that he is the latter. The effect is usually cut in production, but Shakespeare leaves the matter in doubt, so that it clouds any sentimental image of a returning prodigal.

ACT V

V.1: The Marseilles scene

Yet another short scene and a further quickening in the action. Painter's story allowed years to pass before Giletta returned to Beltramo; Shakespeare's stage allows no delay, and keeps the unmasking of Parolles closely associated with that of the Count. The three women, 'with two attendants', have been travelling round the clock, and Helena is in the lead as they enter with their baggage weary from the road: 'But this exceeding posting day and night / Must wear your spirits low . . .' They have reached

France—'a street in Marseilles', as the old editors have it, and seagulls were heard in 1981—and Helena is in a great hurry to find the King.

A Gentleman, or, in the Folio, 'a gentle astringer' (falconer), happens by, and Payne's actor carried a falcon on his wrist as identification. He is also recognisable by his court dress, since Helena no sooner sees him than she exclaims, 'In happy time! / This man may help me to his Majesty's ear.' Nunn had thoughtfully used him to push the King's wheelchair. She immediately asks him to take the King 'this poor petition' (it will turn out to be Diana's), only to learn that he has just left. Another obstacle.

> Gentleman. The King's not here.
> Helena.   Not here, sir?

Payne's Widow and Diana both repeated, 'Not here?', with tired despair in their voices, and Helena comforts them: 'All's Well That Ends Well yet.' However, the Gentleman conveniently reports that the King has gone on his way to Rousillon; Payne's ladies repeated, 'Rousillon?' Conveniently again, the Gentleman is going to that very place, and agrees to take the letter.

The scene is over almost as soon as it has begun: 'We must to horse again', and, to the attendants, 'Go, go, provide', and the little group of women is gone.

V.2: Parolles returns

Parolles's story is briefly developed in another light-hearted scene. He too has a letter he wishes delivered at court, and has evidently travelled to Rousillon also. His former foppish elegance of dress, however, is missing, and he is almost unrecognisable through his mud-stained rags. Clive Swift played a trombone like some street musician: 'I am now, sir, muddied in Fortune's mood, and smell somewhat strong of her strong displeasure.' In this low condition, he treats the Clown with new deference—'Good Monsieur Lavache'—and Lavache takes the opportunity to invent a series of dirty puns at Parolles's expense, backing off and holding his nose: 'Prithee, allow the wind.' ... 'Prithee, get thee further.' And with the entrance of Lafeu, Lavache skips off, Bridges-Adams's clown playing his pipe.

Lafeu does not at first recognise the new Parolles; he takes him for a beggar and tosses him a coin: 'There's a cardecue for you.' But as Lafeu pushes the apparition away—'I am for other business'—Parolles persists.

Parolles. I beseech your honour to hear me one single word.
Lafeu. You beg a single penny more; come, you shall ha't; save your word (*tossing another coin*).
Parolles. My name, my good lord, is Parolles.
Lafeu. You beg more than word then. Cox my passion! give me your hand. How does your drum?

Lafeu shares our amazement at what he sees, but a trumpet sounds, and he hurries off to greet the King, with Parolles on his heels: 'Though you are a fool and a knave, you shall eat. Go to; follow.'

V.3.1-128: Bertram winning and losing

The time of reckoning for Bertram, and of triumph for Helena, has come. V.3 is a long ordeal for the Count, heaping revelation upon revelation, a kind of trial scene that the audience has been waiting for. Bertrand Evans calls it a 'tortuous dénouement', with each twist a clever surprise, and yet no surprise, for the audience. Shakespeare could easily have settled the business with his customary fifth-act aplomb, but in *All's Well* he chooses to play the cards carefully one by one—not, I think, to imply a Helena teasing, torturing or degrading Bertram, but to complete the realistic portrait of his man for our pleasure. This harsh treatment does not, of course, preclude our seeing the last scene as a final example of Helena's special powers, 'curing' Bertram by manipulating people and rings and an unborn child. She is notably offstage for most of the scene, and she has only twelve lines at the very end, but we feel her constant presence among the chief participants.

This last scene is certainly not perfunctory, an example of poor workmanship, as has sometimes been claimed. In performance, it is a gripping piece of theatre without parallel in the other comedies. In her *Shakespeare Quarterly* article, Muriel St Clare Byrne confirms that it is 'demonstrably and brilliantly successful on the stage' (p. 557), and in the production she saw at

Stratford-upon-Avon, Guthrie aimed at a visual contrast between the first scene and the last, a spirit of life and affirmation replacing the smell of death with which the play opened: 'We shall return, but not to the deserted garden: instead, life will flow back to the great house, as the heir comes home and the King comes to Rousillon. Again there is the bustle and excitement. The great state room, shut up since Rousillon became a house of mourning, is made ready under our eyes' (p. 559). In *Shakespeare Survey 31*, Roger Warren wrote that at Stratford, Ontario David Jones banished his wintry scenes with 'touches of spring green, sunny light, and soft cream colours for the clothes of the Countess and Helena' (p. 145). Nunn's courtiers wore light flannels and the King a white Panama hat. With the return to Rousillon, the whole style of the performance is to be light-footed, refreshing.

The same flourish of trumpets that called Lafeu offstage now brings on the King, together with the Countess and Lafeu. The King will lead the lady to her seat—'My honour'd lady'— equalising them in honour due. The older generation has entered talking about the young, and now is to sit in judgement upon them. With a pleasant irony for the audience, which knows rather more of the truth, the talk is of Helena as a 'lost jewel' and of Bertram as 'mad in folly'. His mother pleads Bertram's case:

> Natural rebellion, done i' th' blaze of youth,
> When oil and fire, too strong for reason's force,
> O'erbears it and burns on.

The King responds benevolently with, 'I have forgiven and fogotten all': the lines are serene, the mood conciliatory. The King sits: the stage is orderly and controlled—'let him approach, / A stranger, no offender'. And before Bertram appears, the King has proposed the match between the Count and Lafeu's daughter, who we learn later is 'fair Maudlin'.

Bertram enters diffidently, remembering the last time he was in the presence of the King. He wears his patch, mark of his fame as a soldier; 'He looks well on't' from Lafeu. He bows or drops to his knee before his sovereign, who finally smiles on him:

> I am not a day of season,
> For thou mayst see a sunshine and a hail
> In me at once. But to the brightest beams
> Distracted clouds give way.

The King has no wish to dwell on the past ('Not one word more of the consumed time') and gives Bertram his hand to kiss. Asked about Maudlin, a tongue-tied Bertram utters a speech of curious and convoluted ambiguity, groping for ideas as he speaks. It seems that from the first he fell in love with Maudlin, but did not dare speak what was in his heart ('Make too bold a herald of my tongue'). Nevertheless, his feelings made him scorn all other faces, finding them 'hideous'. We need not believe any of this—in his *The Unfortunate Comedy*, Joseph Price points out that Bertram speaks of Maudlin with the same affected language with which he approached Diana (p. 169). However that may be, he explains how he came to reject Helena:

> Thence it came
> That she whom all men prais'd, and whom myself,
> Since I have lost, have lov'd, was in mine eye
> The dust that did offend it.

Bertram's appeal for understanding at least takes in his mother and the King, who, after a suitable homily in royal couplets, dismisses Helena from his mind and is ready to bless 'our widower's second marriage-day'. In Guthrie's productions, the Countess warmly kissed her son, and his friends in court roundly shook his hand.

The stage is still calm, but it is the calm before the storm. Bertram has been forgiven by the old people, but two rings wait to change the course of his fortunes, together with the two women who had them. He will lie hastily, desperately, so that lies will compound lies and each temporary solution will be displaced by another to the end. For Harold S. Wilson in 'Dramatic Emphasis in *All's Well That Ends Well*', there must be 'a necessary sense of growing pressure on Bertram, of his assurance gradually undermined, until his pride is ready to break' (p. 237).

It adds to his disgrace if fair Maudlin is actually present on the stage, his next possible victim, but even if she is not, disaster will spring from the very idea of marrying her. The King urges Bertram to give his new bride-to-be an 'amorous token', and the girl's father also calls for a favour 'to sparkle in the spirits of my daughter'. Thus it is that Bertram produces the same ring that Helena had from the King and gave Bertram in the night. He gives it to Lafeu, and suddenly a chill falls over the stage. From Lafeu,

> By my old beard,
> And ev'ry hair that's on't, Helen, that's dead,
> Was a sweet creature; such a ring as this,
> The last that e'er I took her leave at court,
> I saw upon her finger.

Bertram is puzzled: 'Hers it was not.' But the King himself takes the ring—he will try it on his finger—and confirms that it was the very one he gave her. We hear his lines, a pleasant irony in our ears,

> when I gave it Helen
> I bade her, if her fortunes ever stood
> Necessitied to help, that by this token
> I would relieve her.

Bertram has unwittingly produced the one ring that will indict him; it was all the time an ace up her sleeve. It is an eloquent plea for help in her absence, and contributes to the impression of her invisible presence on the stage.

Bertram begins an elaborate lie about being thrown the ring from a casement window by a noble lady of Florence. The King listens in disbelief and grows angry; he moves irritably on his throne: ' 'Twas mine, 'twas Helen's, / Whoever gave it you.' She would never have parted with it: 'Confess 'twas hers, and by what rough enforcement / You got it from her.' In the *New Arden Shakespeare* edition, G. K. Hunter observes that the King's lines are increasingly disjointed, expressing his 'wild and whirling thoughts' (p. 135). Bertram breaks away guiltily on, 'She never saw it', and the King doubtless rises on 'as I love mine honour'. Suspicion grows quickly that the Count has killed his wife—murmurs round the stage—and before a horrified court he is marched off between the guards, protesting ironically,

> If you shall prove
> This ring was ever hers, you shall as easy
> Prove that I husbanded her bed in Florence.

V.3.129-298: Diana calls Bertram's bluff

Who should now appear but the 'gentle astringer' with Diana's letter. She has been following the King on his journey to

Rousillon, and has missed him four or five times. The King reads the letter aloud.

> Upon his many protestations to marry me when his wife was dead, I blush to say it, he won me. Now is the Count Rousillon a widower; his vows are forfeited to me, and my honour's paid to him. He stole from Florence, taking no leave, and I follow him to his country for justice. Grant it me, O King! in you it best lies; otherwise a seducer flourishes, and a poor maid is undone.
>
> DIANA CAPILET.

A third young woman? It is a shocking indictment, and Diana herself has not yet appeared. Bertram's former lie grows worse. Lafeu promptly disowns his prospective son-in-law and Bertram is recalled for further interrogation.

> *King.*   I am afeard the life of Helen, lady,
>   Was foully snatch'd.
> *Countess.*   Now, justice on the doers!

The Count returns, but before he can find words to answer the new accusation, Diana appears in person with her mother. Diana kneels, and the Widow curtsies behind her. Guthrie added to the suspense by putting his Diana, Priscilla Morgan, in a veil, and to the comedy by having a rheumatic Widow, Angela Baddeley, need help to get up again. Bertram swings round, sees them and moves away in some alarm. Diana has now become the surrogate Helena, while Helena herself shields her modesty by remaining mysteriously absent.

Confronted by the two Florentine women, Bertram has his back to the wall. Diana walks boldly across to him, and even takes him by the hand:

> *Diana.*   Why do you look so strange upon your wife?
> *Bertram.* She's none of mine, my lord.

His laugh is nervous as he tries to move past her to address the King. But this new Diana is inspired, and faces Bertram again:

> If you shall marry,
> You give away this hand, and that is mine;
> You give away heaven's vows, and those are mine;
> You give away myself, which is known mine.

She seems by this to speak for Helena herself. Priscilla Morgan here unveiled, and Guthrie's court stirred and whispered.

Bertram's immediate defence is to abuse her with his tongue, vainly appealing to the King like one nobleman to another: 'My lord, this is a fond and desp'rate creature / Whom sometime I have laugh'd with.' The King rises and turns away: he is far from convinced. With an even greater show of courage, Diana turns to him and demands directly,

> Good my lord,
> Ask him upon his oath if he does think
> He had not my virginity.

She carefully conceals the truth by her choice of words, and Bertram can only renew his attack upon her reputation: 'She's impudent, my lord, / And was a common gamester to the camp.' But Diana chooses this moment to produce the second ring, the family heirloom given him by the Countess on his departure for the war. Now it is that lady's turn to examine the evidence. She takes the ring from the King, identifies it and gives it back to Diana—'This is his wife: / That ring's a thousand proofs.' If by now the audience is confused by the abundance of rings, and who gave which to whom, it sees the import of each in the faces of the King and the Countess—and in Bertram's bewilderment and panic.

Threatened next with further testimony from Parolles, a man who no longer has reason to wish him well, Bertram now reverses himself and admits that he slept with Diana and gave her the ring:

> Certain it is I lik'd her,
> And boarded her i' th' wanton way of youth.
> She knew her distance, and did angle for me,
> Madding my eagerness with her restraint.

The case against him is growing. He is on the defensive, and nervously moves away from stage centre. He did not reckon with this spirited girl and the encouragement given her by her mother. Diana attacks again: 'You that have turn'd off a first so noble wife / May justly diet me.' To turn the screw still more, she demands her own ring back. Another ring?

Bertram.	I have it not.
King.	What ring was yours, I pray you?
Diana.	Sir, much like
	The same upon your finger.

[111]

Her lines are strong and firm, and she stands as the implacable accuser, although Cheryl Campbell was pleasantly amused by her new role.

Bertram's 'I do confess the ring was hers' is timed to coincide with the entrance of Parolles. The Count is cornered, and has nothing more to say besides the truth. Everyone on stage is amazed at the confession—'sensation' is entered in Bridges-Adams's prompt-book—and everyone's eyes are on him. Like a shying horse, he 'boggles shrewdly'. And Parolles's wit serves only to damn him the more:

> *Parolles.* Faith, sir, he did love her; but how?
> *King.* How, I pray you?
> *Parolles.* He did love her, sir, as a gentleman loves a woman.
> *King.* How is that?
> *Parolles.* He lov'd her, sir, and lov'd her not.

Parolles remains abject and on his knees, but he is clearly recovering his talent as a jester, and the court laughs. He is pleased to play the clown once more, and the tone of the scene shifts effortlessly between the serious and the comic.

The King returns to the mystery of the ring he gave Helena, and the audience enjoys its superior knowledge as Diana answers his questions with a pert confidence:

> *King.* This ring, you say, was yours?
> *Diana.*   Ay, my good lord.
> *King.* Where did you buy it? Or who gave it you?
> *Diana.* It was not given me, nor I did not buy it.
> *King.* Who lent it you?
> *Diana.*   It was not lent me neither.
> *King.* Where did you find it then?
> *Diana.*   I found it not.
> *King.* If it were yours by none of all these ways,
>   How could you give it him?

Lafeu's exasperation speaks for all—'This woman's an easy glove, my lord; she goes off and on at pleasure'—and the court laughs again. Angela Baddeley as the Widow cried, 'Shame!', and, according to Muriel St Clare Byrne, launched herself into a scuffle 'like an infuriated Yorkshire terrier'. Finally the King loses all patience: he decides that Diana is 'some common customer' and orders her to prison. Nevertheless, as frightened as the girl is, she breaks away and stands her ground; Priscilla Morgan actually threw herself down and clasped the King's leg.

The mystery thickens, and her final couplets only add to the puzzle as she turns on Bertram one last time:

> Though yet he never harm'd me, here I quit him.
> He knows himself my bed he hath defil'd;
> And at that time he got his wife with child.
> Dead though she be, she feels her young one kick;
> So there's my riddle: one that's dead is quick.

'I quit him' is ambiguously both positive and negative, both 'I acquit him' and 'I pay him back', and a sarcastic little curtsy would nicely fit the line as well as the riddle. Then, as if her whole performance is a careful piece of stage-management and her speech a prepared cue for a magical effect, Diana completes her assignment with a big gesture upstage.

V.3.299-333: The reconciliation

'Behold the meaning', and the Widow of Florence leads in Helena herself. The Widow's action will break the tension, as did Angela Baddeley, who, in Muriel St Clare Byrne's description, 'with ruffled dignity and set face and pursed lips, the embodiment of pained affront, hobbled doggedly across the full width of the stage to fetch Helena' (p. 567). At least Bertram is not a murderer, only a wife-hater. Helena does not actually produce his offspring, merely appears to be pregnant, unlike the Giletta of Painter's story, who produces twins. Guthrie had her veiled like his Diana, and the Willman and Houseman productions, with steps on the stage, brought her down from on high, a heavenly descent. She curtsies to the King, and the court again stands amazed—'sensation' again from Bridges-Adams. She and Shakespeare have arranged a timely entrance after her long absence from the stage. 'Is't real that I see?' asks the King, and Guthrie's Helena unveiled.

> No, my good lord;
> 'Tis but the shadow of a wife you see,
> The name and not the thing.

Although she appears to speak to the King, she directs her voice over her shoulder to Bertram, and in Nunn's production Harriet Walter did not take her eyes off him.

In the television production the camera passed round the faces of the onlookers, and G. K. Hunter described the effect in a paper for the International Shakespeare Congress of 1981:

On the stage, as the tension builds up through the intrigue, the reservation of Helena for a miraculous, knot-cutting entry places an intolerable burden on that entry: can one simple step through the door cause all this? *We* see her as she is and not as she is received. The television production solved the problem, brilliantly I thought, by concealing the entry. The family and its supporters have lined up imperceptibly, facing the door through which Diana is being taken to prison. At the door she stops and pleads her final stay of execution ... As the cast looks through the door music begins to play. 'Behold the meaning,' says Diana. But the camera does not allow us to behold. Instead it does what the camera does best—it shows us a set of mouths and eyes. As it tracks along the line we are made witness to a series of inner sunrises, as face after face responds to the miracle and lights up with understanding and relief. I confess to finding it a very moving experience. (*Shakespeare Quarterly*, vol. 33, no. 3, autumn 1982, p. 276)

By this device, of course, the stage's focus on Bertram is somewhat dispersed.

That gentleman capitulates immediately. It is a moment for the actor to summon all of Bertram's guilt into a word, a sound: 'Both, both; O pardon!' So he breaks. Gwilym and Franks were on their knees on the floor. If he is no saint, Walter King insists in 'Shakespeare's Mingled Yarn', he at least is human (p. 42). And for those who think this utterance insufficient to meet the momentous occasion, Gervinus in his *Commentaries* of 1852 emphasised the difference between reading this line and seeing it performed on the stage: 'The case is entirely different when, in the acted Bertram ... from the whole bearing of the brusque man, [spectators] perceive what the one word "pardon" signified in his mouth, when they see his breast heave at the last appearance of Helena bringing ease to his conscience' (quoted by F. E. Halliday, *Shakespeare and His Critics*, p. 430). Bertram kneels to Helena, and she raises him to his feet again. Angela Baddeley smiled a 'kind, contented little smile'. Finally, Helena indicates the fulfilment of the two conditions her husband had set her: she points to the ring the Countess is holding, and quotes from Bertram's letter:

There is your ring,
And look you, here's your letter. This it says:

> 'When from my finger you can get this ring,
> And are by me with child,' &c. This is done.
> Will you be mine now you are doubly won?

For the '&c' Payne inserted, 'Then call me husband'; nowadays Helena will touch her stomach. She does not stand in triumph, for her love is humble; it is enough that her humility has proved stronger than his pride. On Guthrie's stage the King and Lafeu both threw up their arms in a gesture of resignation.

Modern literary critics find Bertram's last rhyming couplet inadequate to demonstrate his conversion: it is too short to show a psychological change of heart, and too long to suggest a miraculous bolt from heaven: 'If she, my liege, can make me know this clearly, / I'll love her dearly, ever, ever dearly.' In her *Shakespeare Quarterly* report on Guthrie's Stratford-upon-Avon production, Muriel St Clare Byrne wrote that 'Bertram has a concluding couplet which is perhaps the worst that any actor could be asked to speak', but she added a corollary: 'I did not hear him speak it . . . I saw nothing but Helena' (p. 557). In *Going to Shakespeare*, J. C. Trewin writes simply, 'It goes better, as so much does, in the theatre' (p. 187). After Bertram's long ordeal, one has the strongest sense that words are now superfluous, and that Shakespeare thought so too.

The play is all but done. Guthrie had Bertram place the ring on Helena's finger; Payne had him kiss her. She then runs to embrace her beloved Countess ('O my dear mother, do I see you living?'). The Countess will kiss them both. Lafeu wipes a tear ('Mine eyes smell onions'), but with a rag produced on demand by Parolles ('Good Tom Drum, lend me a handkercher'), a line which prompted a comment from Joseph Price in *The Unfortunate Comedy*: 'How subtly does Shakespeare improve Parolles's fate!' (p. 170). Finally, in a last benevolent gesture, the King offers a husband for Diana to choose. General laughter, since his offer conjures up an image of another Bertram setting new conditions for another Helena, and the story could metadramatically begin all over again. So the play dissolves in fairy-tale rhymes as its title is again invoked: 'All yet seems well; and if it end so meet, / The bitter past, more welcome is the sweet.' In 1981, Bertram and Helena once again waltzed slowly in ironic silhouette, tentatively touching hands before they made their exit without kissing.

In his review of the Barbican production in 1982, Roger Warren reported that Bertram and Helena had introduced a quite subtle indication of their feelings through the use of their hands. In the scene of choosing a husband, she had tried to prevent the King from joining their hands, and when she made her final appearance, Bertram 'went to take her hand, but didn't actually do so; instead he spoke that cryptic, conditional couplet. This wary meeting between husband and wife contrasted strikingly with Helena's intensely moving reunion with the Countess . . . Left alone, Bertram and Helena walked upstage together, their hands still apart, the final image of an unequal marriage. This ending could be presented in all its unsentimental complexity because it had been so thoroughly prepared for' (*Shakespeare Quarterly*, 34.1, spring 1983, p. 80).

In the BBC TV edition of *All's Well*, John Wilders, who clearly does not like the play, believes that, judging from the King's couplet, he 'looks to the future with guarded optimism' and that the audience 'very likely leaves the theatre bewildered' (p. 10). If that is the case, then it has not felt the unsentimental thrust of the drama. Should that 'seems' and that 'if' raise doubts about the successful outcome of the match, it is because the play has been a folk tale composed of many harsh and realistic elements. The hesitant note in the Epilogue even suggests an ironic wink at the audience, and Barton made the point by having Ian Richardson slap Estelle Kohler on the back at their final exit. The flourish of the King's trumpets and the swelling music may seem to comfort us home, but the play sustains its wry tone to the end. G. B. Shaw would have called it 'an anti-romantic comedy'.

BIBLIOGRAPHY.
BOOKS AND ARTICLES

Adams, John F., 'All's Well That Ends Well: The Paradox of Procreation', Shakespeare Quarterly, XII, 1961, 261-70.

Arthos, John, 'The Comedy of Generation', Essays in Criticism, V.2, April 1955, 97-117.

Babb, Lawrence, The Elizabethan Malady, East Lansing, 1951.

Barton, Anne, ed., All's Well That Ends Well in The Riverside Shakespeare, ed. G. Blakemore Evans, Boston, 1974.

BBC TV, All's Well That Ends Well, London, 1981.

Bradbrook, M. C., 'Virtue Is the True Nobility: a Study of the Structure of All's Well', Review of English Studies, 1.4, October 1950, 289-301.

Brown, John Russell, Shakespeare and His Comedies, London, 1957, ch. VII.

Byrne, Muriel St Clare, 'The Shakespeare Season at the Old Vic, 1958-59 and Stratford-upon-Avon, 1959', Shakespeare Quarterly, X.4, autumn 1959, 556-67.

Calderwood, James L., 'The Mingled Yarn of All's Well', Journal of English and Germanic Philology, LXII, 1963, 61-76.

—— 'Styles of Knowing in All's Well', Modern Language Quarterly, XXV.3, September 1964, 272-94.

Carter, Albert Howard, 'In Defense of Bertram', Shakespeare Quarterly, VII.1, winter 1956, 21-31.

Coleridge, Samuel Taylor, Shakespearean Criticism, ed. T. M. Raysor, London, 1930.

David, Richard, 'Plays Pleasant and Plays Unpleasant', Shakespeare Survey 8, 1955, 132-8.

Davies, Robertson, Renown at Stratford, Toronto, 1953.

Davies, Thomas, Dramatic Miscellanies, London, 1783.

Ellis-Fermor, U., Shakespeare the Dramatist, London, 1961, 128-32.

Evans, Bertrand, Shakespeare's Comedies, London, 1960, ch.V.

Everett, Barbara, ed., All's Well That Ends Well (New Penguin Shakespeare), Harmondsworth, 1970.

Goldsmith, Robert H., Wise Fools in Shakespeare, East Lansing, 1955.

Gordon, George, Shakespearian Comedy, London, 1944.

Guthrie, Tyrone, A Life in the Theatre, New York, 1959.

Halio, Jay L., 'All's Well That Ends Well', Shakespeare Quarterly, XV.1, winter 1964, 33-43.

Halliday, F. E., Shakespeare and His Critics, London, 1949

Halstead. William P., *Shakespeare As Spoken*, Ann Arbor, 1979, vol. 4.

Hapgood, Robert, 'The Life of Shame: Parolles and *All's Well*', *Essays in Criticism*, XV.3, July 1965, 269-78.

Hazlitt, William, *Characters of Shakespeare's Plays*, London, 1920.

Hunter, G. K., ed., *All's Well That Ends Well* (*New Arden Shakespeare*), London, 1959.

Hunter, Robert G., *Shakespeare and the Comedy of Forgiveness*, New York, 1965, 106-31.

Johnson, Samuel, in *The Yale Edition of the Works*, New Haven, 1968, vol. VII.

King, Walter N., 'Shakespeare's "Mingled Yarn" ', *Modern Language Quarterly*, XXI.1, March 1960, 33-44.

Kirsch, Arthur, *Shakespeare and the Experience of Love*, Cambridge, 1981, ch. 5.

Knight, G. Wilson, *The Sovereign Flower*, London, 1958, 95-160.

La Guardia, Eric, 'Chastity, Regeneration, and World Order in *All's Well That Ends Well*' in *Myth and Symbol*, ed. Bernice Slote, 1963, 119-32.

Lawrence, W. W., *Shakespeare's Problem Comedies*, New York, 1931, ch. II.

Leech, Clifford, 'The Theme of Ambition in *All's Well That Ends Well*', *A Journal of English Literary History*, 21.1, March 1954, 17-29.

Muir, Kenneth, *Shakespeare's Sources*, London, 1957, 97-101.

Nagarajan, S., 'The Structure of *All's Well That Ends Well*', *Essays in Criticism*, X.1, January 1960, 24-31.

Parrott, T.M., *Shakespearean Comedy*, New York, 1949.

Price, Joseph G., *The Unfortunate Comedy: A Study of 'All's Well That Ends Well' and Its Critics*, Toronto, 1968.

Quiller-Couch, A., ed., *All's Well That Ends Well* (*New Cambridge Shakespeare*), Cambridge, 1929.

Ranald, Margaret L., 'The Betrothals of *All's Well That Ends Well*', *Huntington Library Quarterly*, XXVI, 1963, 179-92.

Rossiter, A. P., *Angel with Horns and Other Shakespeare Lectures*, ed. Graham Storey, London, 1961, ch. V.

Schlegel, A. W., *Lectures on Dramatic Art and Literature*, trans. John Black, London, 1883.

Schoff, Francis G., 'Claudio, Bertram, and a Note on Interpretation', *Shakespeare Quarterly*, X.1, 1959, 11-23.

Shattuck, Charles H., *The Shakespeare Promptbooks: a Descriptive Catalogue*, Urbana, 1965.

Shaw, G. B., *Our Theatres in the Nineties*, London, 1932.

Shenstone, William, *Letters*, ed. Marjorie Williams, London, 1939.

Speaight, Robert, *William Poel and the Elizabethan Revival*, London, 1954.

Stoll, E. E., *From Shakespeare to Joyce*, New York, 1944. ch. XIII.

Tillyard, E. M. W., *Shakespeare's Problem Plays*, Toronto, 1949, 89-117.

Trewin, J. C., *Going to Shakespeare*, London, 1978.

—— *Shakespeare on the English Stage, 1900-1964*, London, 1964.

Turner, Robert Y., 'Dramatic Conventions in *All's Well That Ends Well*', *Publications of the Modern Language Association*, LXXV, 1960, 497-502.

Van Doren, Mark, *Shakespeare* (Anchor Books ed.), New York, 1939.

Warren, Roger, 'Comedies and Histories at Two Stratfords, 1977', *Shakespeare Survey* 31, 1978, 141-53.

—— 'Does It End Well? Helena, Bertram and the Sonnets', *Shakespeare Survey* 22, 1969, 79-92.

Wheeler, Richard P, *Shakespeare's Development and the Problem Comedies: Turn and Counter-Turn*, Berkeley, 1981, ch. II.

Wickham, Glynne, *Early English Stages*, London, 1981, vol. III.

Wilson, Harold S., 'Dramatic Emphasis in *All's Well That Ends Well*', *Huntington Library Quarterly*, XIII.3, May 1950, 217-40.

APPENDIX

A. Twentieth-century productions

1916	F. R. Benson	Stratford-upon-Avon
1920	William Poel	Ethical Church, Bayswater
1921	Robert Atkins	Old Vic
1922	W. Bridges-Adams	Stratford-upon-Avon
1927	Barry Jackson	Birmingham Repertory Theatre
1935	Ben Iden Payne	Stratford-upon-Avon
1937	Maxwell Sholes	Pasadena Playhouse, California
1940	Robert Atkins	Vaudeville Theatre, London
1953	Tyrone Guthrie	Stratford, Ontario
1953	Michael Benthall	Old Vic
1955	Noël Willman	Stratford-upon-Avon
1959	Tyrone Guthrie	Stratford-upon-Avon
1959	John Houseman	Stratford, Connecticut
1967/1968	John Barton	Stratford-upon-Avon/ Aldwych Theatre, London
1975	Jonathan Miller	Greenwich Theatre
1977	David Jones	Stratford, Ontario
1980	Elijah Moshinsky	BBC TV
1981/1982	Trevor Nunn	Stratford-upon-Avon/ Barbican Theatre, London

B. Major productions: principal casts

1916 (23 April). Director: F. R. Benson

Helena	Florence Glossop-Harris	*Bertram*	Murray Kinnell
		Countess	Constance Benson
Parolles	F.R. Benson	*Lafeu*	H.O. Nicholson
King	James Dale	*Widow*	Rose Edouin
Lavache	Christian Morrow	*Diana*	Dorothie Pidcock

[120]

1921 (28 November). Director: Robert Atkins

Helena	Jane Bacon	*Bertram*	Alan Walls
Parolles	Ernest Milton	*Countess*	Florence Buckton
King	Wilfred Walter	*Lafeu*	Rupert Harvey
Lavache	Andrew Leigh	*Diana*	Esther Whitehouse

1922 (23 April). Director: W. Bridges-Adams

Helena	Maureen Shaw	*Bertram*	Maurice Colbourne
Parolles	Baliol Holloway	*Countess*	Dorothy Green
King	William Stack	*Lafeu*	Stanley Lathbury
Lavache	John Maclean	*Widow*	Ethel Carrington
	Diana	Olive Walter	

1935 (23 April). Director: Ben Iden Payne. Designer: Lloyd Weninger

Helena	Jean Shepeard	*Bertram*	Raymond Raikes
Parolles	Roy Emerton	*Countess*	Catherine Lacey
King	Neil Porter	*Lafeu*	Stanley Howlett
Lavache	Kenneth Wicksteed	*Widow*	Barbara Gott
	Diana	Rosamund Merivale	

1940 (3 October). Director: Robert Atkins

Helena	Patricia Tucker	*Bertram*	Peter Glenville
Parolles	Esme Percy	*Countess*	Catherine Lacey
King	Ernest Milton	*Lafeu*	Robert Atkins
	Lavache	Jerry Verno	

1953 (14 July). Director: Tyrone Guthrie. Designer: Tanya Moiseiwitsch

Helena	Irene Worth	*Bertram*	Donald Harron
Parolles	Douglas Campbell	*Countess*	Eleanor Stuart
King	Alec Guiness	*Lafeu*	Michael Bates
Widow	Amelia Hall	*Diana*	Beatrice Lennard

1953 (15 September). Director: Michael Benthall
Designer: Osbert Lancaster. Music: Gordon Jacob

Helena	Claire Bloom	*Bertram*	John Neville
Parolles	Michael Hordern	*Countess*	Fay Compton
King	Laurence Hardy	*Lafeu*	William Squire
Widow	Viola Lyel	*Diana*	Gwen Cherrell

1955 (26 April). Director: Noël Willman
Designer: Mariano Andreu. Lighting: Peter Streult

Helena	Joyce Redman	*Bertram*	Michael Denison
Parolles	Keith Michell	*Countess*	Rosalind Atkinson
King	Alan Webb	*Lafeu*	Ralph Michael
Lavache	Edward Atienza	*Widow*	Nancye Stewart
	Diana	Jill Dixon	

1959 (21 April). Director: Tyrone Guthrie
Designer: Tanya Moiseiwitsch. Lighting: Maurice Daniels

Helena	Zoe Caldwell	*Bertram*	Edward de Souza

Parolles	Cyril Luckham	*Countess*	Edith Evans
King	Robert Hardy	*Lafeu*	Anthony Nicholls
Widow	Angela Baddeley	*Diana*	Priscilla Morgan

1959 (1 August). Director: John Houseman

Helena	Nancy Wickwire	*Bertram*	John Ragin
Parolles	Richard Waring	*Countess*	Aline MacMahon
King	Larry Gates	*Lafeu*	Will Geer
Widow	Sada Thompson	*Diana*	Barbara Barrie

1967 (1 June). Director: John Barton
Designer: Timothy O'Brien. Lighting: John Bradley

Helena	Estelle Kohler/	*Bertram*	Ian Richardson
	Lynn Farleigh (1968)	*Parolles*	Clive Swift
Countess	Catherine Lacey	*King*	Sebastian Shaw
Lafeu	Brewster Mason	*Lavache*	Ian Hogg
Widow	Elizabeth Spriggs	*Diana*	Helen Mirren

1975 (10 July). Director: Jonathan Miller

Helena	Penelope Wilton	*Bertram*	David Horovitch
Parolles	David Frith	*Countess*	Sylvia Coleridge
King	Joseph O'Connor	*Lafeu*	John Arnat

1977 (8 June). Director: David Jones. Designer: Tanya Moiseiwitsch
Lighting: Gil Wechsler. Music: Louis Applebaum

Helena	Martha Henry	*Bertram*	Nicholas Pennell
Parolles	Richard Monette	*Countess*	Margaret Tyzack
King	William Hutt	*Lafeu*	Leslie Yeo
Lavache	Tom Wood	*Widow*	Florence Paterson
	Diana	Barbara Stephen	

1980 (recorded 23-29 July). Director: Elijah Moshinsky
Costume: Colin Lavers
Designer: David Myerscough-Jones. Lighting: John Summers

Helena	Angela Down	*Bertram*	Ian Charleson
Parolles	Peter Jeffrey	*Countess*	Celia Johnson
King	Donald Sinden	*Lafeu*	Michael Hordern
Lavache	Paul Brooke	*Widow*	Rosemary Leach
	Diana	Pippa Guard	

1981 (11 November), 1982 (29 May). Director: Trevor Nunn.
Designer: John Gunter. Lighting: Robert Bryan. Music: Guy Woolfenden.

Helena	Harriet Walter	*Bertram*	Mike Gwilym/
Parolles	Stephen Moore		Philip Franks
King	John Franklyn Robbins	*Countess*	Peggy Ashcroft
Lavache	Geoffrey Hutchings	*Lafeu*	Robert Eddison
Diana	Cheryl Campbell	*Widow*	Gillian Webb

[122]

INDEX